The Heart of School Leadership

The Heart of School Leadership

What Education Leaders Need to Create a Thriving School Community

Mary Louise Stahl

ROWMAN & LITTLEFIELD
Lanham • Boulder • New York • London

Published by Rowman & Littlefield
An imprint of The Rowman & Littlefield Publishing Group, Inc.
4501 Forbes Boulevard, Suite 200, Lanham, Maryland 20706
www.rowman.com
86-90 Paul Street, London EC2A 4NE, United Kingdom

Copyright © 2023 by Mary Louise Stahl

All rights reserved. No part of this book may be reproduced in any form or by any electronic or mechanical means, including information storage and retrieval systems, without written permission from the publisher, except by a reviewer who may quote passages in a review.

British Library Cataloguing in Publication Information Available

Library of Congress Cataloging-in-Publication Data

Names: Stahl, Mary Louise, 1960– author.
Title: The heart of school leadership : what education leaders need to create a thriving school community / Mary Louise Stahl.
Description: Lanham, Maryland : Rowman & Littlefield, [2023] | Includes bibliographical references. | Summary: "The Heart of School Leadership focuses on 50 areas that school leaders need to think about in order to nurture a cohesive school community"— Provided by publisher.
Identifiers: LCCN 2022038621 (print) | LCCN 2022038622 (ebook) | ISBN 9781475868555 (Cloth) | ISBN 9781475868562 (Paperback) | ISBN 9781475868579 (epub)
Subjects: LCSH: Educational leadership—Philosophy. | School administrators—Conduct
 of life. | School environment—Social aspects.
Classification: LCC LB2805 .S7428 2023 (print) | LCC LB2805 (ebook) | DDC 371.2/011—dc23/eng/20220930
LC record available at https://lccn.loc.gov/2022038621
LC ebook record available at https://lccn.loc.gov/2022038622

To handle yourself, use your head; to handle others, use your heart.

—Eleanor Roosevelt

Contents

Preface	ix
Acknowledgments	xiii
Introduction	xv
PART I: HEART: OTHERS, SELF-CARE, CHARACTER	**1**
Chapter 1: Others	3
Chapter 2: Self-Care	13
Chapter 3: Character	19
PART II: HEAD: BOOK SMART, STREET SMART	**23**
Chapter 4: Book Smart	25
Chapter 5: Street Smart	31
PART III: HEAD AND HEART: TEACHERS, STUDENTS, EVERYONE	**37**
Chapter 6: Teachers	39
Chapter 7: Students	49
Chapter 8: Everyone	55
Conclusion	59
Appendix: Red Journal Entries and Musings	61
Epilogue: Voices from the Field	73

References 81
About the Author 83

Preface

After finishing my fifteenth year as a school leader, I came upon a personal essay I wrote after working as a substitute principal for one year at a public elementary school. I have since finished my PhD in Educational Leadership, started teaching college as an adjunct, and also continued working as an assistant principal, in a position I took because I thought that "middle management" would be an easier load while I completed my doctorate. For anyone who has worked in a "middle management" position, I can hear you laughing.

Ok, so it wasn't easier, but I learned a lot, and it was a step I had to take. So I decided to revisit this essay, and possibly add new insights and new lessons. I also realized that almost everything I described here has continued to be my leadership foundation, and goes back to my high school yearbook quote from Eleanor Roosevelt: "To handle yourself, use your head; to handle others, use your heart." Hopefully something here will be useful to anyone embarking on a job, and actually a life, as a school leader. Here is the beginning of the essay:

> I am feeling overwhelmed, puzzled, humbled and, to be honest, slightly confused. I just spent a year as the substitute principal of a public suburban elementary school with 600 students (Kindergarten through 5th grade) and 100 faculty and staff. I had already been the principal of a private all girls' high school for three years, so I knew the job, and did it well. Well, the best you can do your first year on the job.
>
> Personally, I thought my job performance was possibly a B, since I spent most of the year learning things as I went, and being reactive rather than proactive–thank God for unbelievable secretaries! I had hoped to stay another year (or forever) to improve my work performance and do everything better the second time around, but since the principal who took a year-long leave of absence decided to return, I did not have that opportunity.
>
> Still, I am grateful. I always strive to be grateful, even when I am disappointed, frustrated, and well, in this case . . . just plain sad. I spent a year

falling in love with a community and culture that I respected and loved, and then it ended.

The part I am overwhelmed and puzzled about is what happened when I left. I was showered with the kindest words I have ever received, the nicest gifts, the sweetest, most tearful speeches and goodbyes, and I am just wondering . . . what am I doing as a leader, and as a person, to be the recipient of all of this? They shared with me that many leaders have come and gone, but have never received this type of goodbye . . . ever.

I am 50 years old, well-educated (one bachelor's degree, two master's degrees, and I'm working on a doctorate degree in Educational Leadership), probably intelligent in some ways, but certainly not as bright as some people, because believe me—I have gaps in my knowledge and skills. I have had a varied range of professional and personal experiences in my life, but I've never even been to Europe. My strong faith in God and a commitment to the "Golden Rule" have made me well-organized and a hard worker, but seriously . . . why all the fuss after only one year?

Yes, it feels good to be so appreciated, even though that was never my objective. But most importantly, based on feedback I received from my staff this past year, as well as when I left other leadership positions, whatever I'm doing seems to affect job performance. So I wonder . . . what is it that I'm doing?

When I left, I was given a red leather-bound journal with a heart embossed on the front. It took me months to muster the emotional strength to read it all, and after I finally did, I wondered who would ever need riches or any other earthly treasure, after they had been given a gift such as this journal. I include some excerpts from my beautiful gift as my qualitative evidence for this brand of leadership, and in an attempt to find clues to help describe it:

"Don't cry because she is gone, smile because she was here." I heard this quote at a memorial service yesterday for a woman who died just nine days shy of her 101st birthday. She was described as an angel on earth—sweet, subdued, and endlessly patient. I knew her well–it was an apt description. Yet, when those words were spoken, it was you who sprang to mind.

At one time or another, I have worked in every school, both public and private, in this district. Over the years, I have worked with more administrators than I can count. Happily, I have been able to work with all of them. So when you came to our school, I expected the experience to be the same. It was.

Here is what I didn't expect. I didn't expect to find a person behind the desk who treated everyone equally, whose warmth was real, and whose joy was freely expressed and meant for all. An administrator's life is not easy. Sometimes it's hard to find a friend, even among your peers.

The experience can toughen a person. You surprised me every day because I saw strength rather than toughness, sincerity rather than guile, and the ability to change a culture. This was one of the hardest years that I have ever had to get through. You were my gift. If I live to be 101 years old myself, I will never forget it. Love, Anonymous.

Please believe that I have included these notes, not to brag or prove something to you, but to illustrate and try to put into concrete words (if that's even possible) how effective school leadership can be accomplished. I have also used these loving notes as a clue to unlock what happened here, and what it is that people appreciate and respond to most. I have dissected their words to try to come up with common threads, to see what worked the best to unify a culture and increase happiness, and thus success, in our jobs.

My leadership experience began with summers working as a counselor and program director at a 4-H camp, and went on to include working as a playground leader, being a waitress (the first lesson in customer service), 12 years as a teacher, eight years managing a group home for disabled adults, and four years as a school principal. Being a good leader is like being a good teacher. You know it when you see it, but it is sometimes difficult to teach or describe.

I think that the practices I picked up over the years came from a place of sincerity, and from who I chose to be as a person, as well as the person my parents, family, and role models helped form. I am still a work in progress. If you don't *feel* like you want to do these things and it doesn't come from the heart, I think you can still *fake* some of them and garner some very positive results. If it's not sincerely done at first, faking it until you make it may eventually help you see the beauty of these practices.

Being a school leader has been one of the highest honors and greatest challenges of my professional and personal career. As is the case with most professions, you (hopefully) earn a degree and get some practice before you accept a full-time position leading a school, or assisting in leading a school. Similar to parenting, you are affecting our most important commodity and investment, which is the lives of our children.

You are entrusted every day with their safety, well-being, academic and emotional success, and, simply put, with how they will navigate and imprint on each other and the world. This responsibility is daunting and far-reaching, and you'll need to partner with other professionals, parents, and guardians to do this vital work.

It's surprising that teachers and school leaders are not paid the same as doctors or professional athletes, but until that happens, you can rely on the satisfaction that comes when you keep kids safe, and teach them skills they can use to live their best lives, to be kind to others, and to be happy. For now, that is pay enough.

Acknowledgments

First of all, this book probably wouldn't exist if I had not experienced an idyllic year as an elementary school principal at Eggert Road Elementary School in Orchard Park, New York. So I need to thank the amazing Joan Thomas, who was both my first leadership mentor and the superintendent who hired me two days before she retired. The teachers, staff, students, and families at Eggert Road were wonderful, and they believed in me, which prompted me to reflect on my leadership style.

My leadership jobs before and after that year also contributed to my experience and perspective, so I am grateful to all the students, teachers, parents, and staff I have had the privilege to work with at my alma mater, Immaculata Academy, and at a school I gave my heart to years ago, St. Francis High School.

This book also wouldn't exist without my son, editor, and friend, Samuel Stahl, who is the best editor I know, and not just because he attended the Columbia Publishing Course and has almost completed his PhD, but because he was born a voracious reader and intellect, and is as kind and empathetic as he is intelligent. I am grateful for the hours he devoted to making this into something it never would have been, even when he was only paid in books.

My husband Tom, the true artist in the family, put up with us at laptops in the kitchen for hours of hilarity and work. He has forever believed that I can do anything, which isn't actually true, but it's nice to have someone who believes that about you. I love you both so much, and of course Joe Fox, too.

My parents, along with my five siblings and their families, are my best friends and supporters, and I am so happy I share my life with them, along with my large, loving extended family on my husband's side. The foundation of my work has always been kindness and faith, cornerstones for living that Chuck and Shirley modeled and taught us—along with dancing! Thank you to Darcy, my best friend since the first day of college, for love and support always. I thank the eight leaders who generously contributed to this work, because I admire all of them, and rely on their insight, advice, and support.

Spending the last 10 years working with Tom Braunscheidel influenced my leadership style greatly, and I am so grateful for his friendship. Lastly, and vitally, I want to thank Tom Koerner and Kira Hall at Rowman & Littlefield. I sent my original manuscript to many publishers, and Tom asked me to rewrite my original work. I initially said no, but a year and a half later, Tom asked again, so I said yes. I am forever grateful that he believed in something I hadn't even written yet. Thank you!

Introduction

This book started out as a completely different project, and was originally part memoir, part strategy book, drawing on 15 years of my experiences as a school leader. When I looked at it objectively, I realized that most of the areas that were different from my formal school leader training and degree had to do with the work of the heart.

Most school administrators decide to begin the work of school leadership and service from an emotional tug, which is similar to wanting to be a teacher. Sometimes you have an unforgettable teacher or principal whom you want to emulate, and sometimes you want to do things better, do things differently. It doesn't matter how you get there; it matters that you begin with the heart, and let it lead most of your work.

Of course, all work cannot be accomplished from an emotional base, but how you navigate our relationships with teachers, students, and parents has to start there. This leadership book is organized into sections that focus on work involving the heart, work involving the head, and work that spans both categories. It's my love song to school leadership. I apologize in advance if some of this seems like common sense, but based on my experiences being supervised and working with school leaders, sadly, it's not.

PART I

Heart: Others, Self-Care, Character

There is a section in the original essay advising school leaders to "do the job, of course." There is so much to this, and it could be a separate book all by itself. Obviously many such books have been written on the subject. Although there are many components to earning a school leadership degree, and putting everything into practice, it is the aspects that are handled with the *heart* that can actually set leaders apart.

This book is not here to diagnose the *why* of that, but only to attempt to articulate what that looks like. There are many leaders who are excellent at everything from legal issues to maintenance issues, and those are all part of the job, but the lens of approaching leadership with a sincere heart can be the most important thing.

Chapter 1

Others

This "journey of the heart" has to begin with a focus on others. The chapter titles of this section are obviously all focused on your treatment of and respect for the other people you will encounter every day as a school leader. Some of these areas may not be touched upon in a leadership course, as there are many important aspects of being a school leader, and some programs might not have time to cover what they might consider the "soft skills" of leadership. This section focuses on the part of leadership that needs the most attention. Otherwise, the other parts won't matter. How you treat others can make or break your leadership.

BE KIND

The most important aspect of being a school leader is being kind . . . to everyone. Often a very small act of kindness can change someone's day, and as school leaders you have the incredible opportunity (or gift) to be kind to everyone you encounter. The opportunity to set a tone of inclusivity and kindness is unique to school leaders. This is obviously important for middle management, too, but it has more impact if you are the principal, president, or head of school. It just does.

Maybe it's because those in higher positions are viewed as having less available time, or possibly more influence. Whatever the reason, that is why it can be such a gift and have such an impact. Research has shown that the number one reason for failure as a school leader is actually poor interpersonal skills,[1] so this belief is not merely based on some Pollyanna philosophy, but sound data.

As an assistant principal, you can stand on your head all day and spit nickels, and it will definitely have an impact, but as a principal, you have more impact and it's farther reaching, and it's so easy you'd think it was top secret classified information, but it's not. It's accessible to all. It's also important to share with students that they may accomplish many things in life and be very successful, but if they aren't kind, those accomplishments don't amount to much. It never hurt anyone to be overly generous—with time, positive feedback, understanding, inclusivity, and empathy. This is the basis for good leadership.

If you're wondering what being kind really means, think back to the *golden rule*, and treating others the way you want to be treated. When you walk into a room, you want someone to acknowledge you, maybe even know your name, and to value what you are contributing or needing at that time. You just crave being seen, in its simplest sense, which can happen when a school leader greets you, shares information with you, or asks you for your opinion. The question that can set a school leader apart from so many others is simply, "What do you think?"

BE REAL

Being "real" seems to be something that is extremely important to teachers and staff, and instead of dissecting the psychology behind it, you need to trust it to be so. To be honest, if anyone in a school community describes you or your style as "real," you may be apt to wonder if that is really a compliment, because when you start to picture this quality and how it could possibly manifest in a professional, or even imagine the iconic childhood character in the book *The Velveteen Rabbit*,[2] it might not be what you're initially striving for.

Nevertheless, it strikes a chord with teachers and staff, families and students, and, well, everyone in your community. So what does it really mean to be "real"?

If you try to dissect the word "real" as it applies to leadership, perhaps it means honest. While most people can all admire ultraprofessional people, it is probably not necessary to put on a fake front in all your waking hours in order to be respected. This is challenging to describe in school leadership interviews because it can't really be . . . it can only be shown, and in some circles, it might even be frowned upon.

Some believe that this style of leadership, where a leader lets their armor down, or is viewed as a "softie," opens you up to being taken advantage of. This simply isn't true. Being real does not mean you are all sunshine and naivete and flowers shooting out of your hinder parts all day. However you wish to define "being real," perhaps one person on your staff will see this as an opportunity to get what they want, but once you address them consistently and fairly, even that will go away.

Another part of being real is being honest: about yourself, but mostly about your staff, and mostly the positives. This can involve giving teachers and staff a sincere, unsolicited compliment, whether in person or via a small note or an email. If you see something positive, and think it won't make a difference, think again. Sometimes you don't know the small effect that small, honest observations can have on people when you speak them out loud. Of course, this practice may need to be adapted depending on the population you are working with, that is, preschool, elementary school, single-gender high school, college, and so forth.

In addition, being chatty and open with your teachers and staff, while still remaining professional, can foster a relaxed, lighthearted environment that will make them feel comfortable and at home. If you can achieve that, the workplace can feel so good that everyone will want to put in extra hours, and be happy to come to school each Monday! If you make a mistake or a fumble, own it, and apologize when you do; that is all part of being a real boss and school leader. You might think you will lose respect by being fallible, but you will actually gain it.

KNOW PEOPLE

It probably sounds simple and obvious, but knowing people is the most important thing, and after speaking to many people about their bosses, it is either not so obvious, or just not valued by leaders. You can have little cooperation without "knowing your team." That being said, whether it comes from a natural curiosity or a conscious desire to make this a priority, it takes work. It may be naturally important to you because of things your parents and family valued, but you will see such dramatic results as a leader, that this too can seem like a well-kept secret.

If you have a natural talent for noticing when people get a haircut or new glasses, or lose two pounds, these details can be used to enhance your leadership style. This can also help you notice when people are upset or a little "off." This gives you the opportunity to ask them about it and support them, simply by acknowledging it. Just like our students when they enter the classroom, staff are always carrying *something* with them, whether good or bad, and they seem to work better when you give them the chance to process it.

As you might know from your days as a teacher, when students enter the classroom, giving them a minute to unload whatever they're carrying can help them focus on the lesson. The same principle applies with staff. At the beginning of each school year, it is powerful to tell your teachers that you value their personal lives and their families, and that only by respecting the personal things we all carry, can we do our best work.

You may be surprised that some teachers will say they haven't heard this before. You can ask them if they have anything they want to "download" or share before you get down to business. You may be surprised by the honest sharing that can occur as a result, and how helpful it is for everyone. After this, it is easier to get to work. Really knowing people and valuing them almost always makes them work harder, do more, and be happier and more content at work. We spend so much of our time working. Why should it be scary and miserable?

If being real doesn't come naturally, you have to work at it. It is helpful to spend some time in the summer before a new job memorizing the yearbook and website so you know peoples' names, and what they do for the school. Once you have the staff down, then move on to the students. It can feel a little odd when you mention to a teacher you've just met that their haircut looks nice (because it's different from their yearbook photo), but it's all worth the time you put in.

If you have already spent many years as a school leader, you may have a lot of names in your brain, just like a teacher with a long career. This can make recall challenging. Sometimes you may run into someone and you can't retrieve the name immediately (it of course comes to you five minutes later), so maybe remembering you loved them, and greeting them as such, is enough. If your experience includes saying the wrong name a few too many times, sometimes it's best to keep quiet.

This kind of preparation gives you control over so much before you begin. It gives you a leg up because the brain can focus on leading, once you have the basics down. If you know who people are and what they do, it makes starting out that much easier. It's also important to know everything you can about a place, such as programs, customs, and initiatives. Sometimes this can even set you apart at a job interview. It's also important to know the mailman, the vendors and delivery people, and all of the support staff, which will be covered in chapter 10. Even if you are naturally nosy and curious, this also takes work, time, and effort.

If you are already someone who lives out these practices, you will have seen the kind of culture this familiarity and kindness creates, and it is worth a little extra time on your part. If you don't truly value people, they won't value you or want to work with you. They will find small ways to criticize you, and that critical narrative can grow, because gossip is sport for some, and the smallest thing will become fodder.

KNOW THEIR FAMILIES

Knowing your staff also includes knowing their families. As soon as you meet someone's parents or children, write down notes so you can study and remember the details. If you don't think this is important, wait until the parents of your PTO (Parent Teacher Organization) president come into the school for the second time and you remember their names.

They will not only feel welcome and appreciated, but they will tell about 50 other people. It is the smallest possible thing you can do to show respect and appreciation for them, and it will pay you and your institution back a hundredfold, thus benefiting the students, which is at the core of all that you are doing.

If you aren't good at remembering names, then you might have to work a little harder at it. You can also ask your secretary, husband, child, or close co-worker to help you out if you are stumped. Just tell them ahead of time to introduce themselves, so the other person says their name. Everyone is human and sometimes messes up, but you have to let that go, too. When you do engage with anyone visiting your school, make sure to give them your full attention.

Don't be distracted, look at your phone, or look around. This is difficult when you are welcoming a large crowd into your school for an event, but do your best. Just keep your interactions short, sincere, and focused, and you will do great. Along with the families of your staff, it's important to write down and acknowledge surgeries, births, deaths, and both celebratory and difficult times. A five-minute stop at a wake or a graduation party goes a very long way when you are the boss.

This may sound horrible, but if you really don't care, then at least try to fake it. Seriously. If you do sincerely care, that is half the work. Also, as noted earlier, this is still very important if you are an assistant principal or work in any capacity as a school leader. It still makes a difference and means something to people. I have heard school leaders say that they are uncomfortable at wakes and funerals. Isn't everyone? It's important to get out of yourself, empathize, and be there for people.

It's usually a good idea to go right when the event begins. For example, if a wake begins at 4:00 p.m., it is acceptable to walk in about five minutes ahead of time. If the family is having a private prayer or moment before the viewing, respectfully wait in the hall. If you arrive when it begins, there won't be a long line. This is a big part of your job as a school leader.

GREET PEOPLE

A principal's office is usually, but not always, "protected" against people just stopping in. You might have a completely open office, but more commonly, one with a "first line of defense" and two or more secretaries, and even a front desk monitor and video that screens visitors. There are advantages and disadvantages to both, but if you truly want to create an open culture and still keep your sanity, you have to develop practices that work for you.

If you have a "protected" office, then this is a sound practice and philosophy: every time you hear a voice, whether you recognize it or not, and especially if it's someone you don't recognize, listen to what they are there for. It is almost always a good idea to step out of your office and greet them. You can introduce yourself and spend two minutes with them, and then retreat back to your office (everyone knows the principal is busy). It will pay you back a million times over.

I think all bosses get used to working on things and being interrupted every 30 seconds or so, and sometimes you may even begin to feel that you can't work without interruptions. Even though stopping your work seems inconvenient, it means a great deal to people. In the way of paperwork, it sometimes works best to save it for after people have left the building, or evenings or weekends, because uninterrupted time is really best for quality writing, and a little quiet time goes much further than a whole day of attempting to work with interruptions. Your work and sanity will be better for it.

Some school leaders plan to close their door and get some work done, but it hardly ever happens; it just doesn't fit the job. People are much more important and interesting, anyhow. Also included in the category of greeting people is being at the door for every big event, and as many small events as you can be. People want to see *you*! This is not so much because you are you (although you are probably fabulous), but for the obvious reason that your attendance shows your investment in what they value most: their children.

GET INVOLVED AND HELP OUT

Later on I describe the style of MBWA, or *Management by Walking Around*[3] and the important part about walking around is that you need to help out. You need to spend time in the trenches and do their jobs a little, too. Throughout your travels you may end up mopping floors, unplugging toilets, wiping noses, tying shoes, giving impromptu hugs, taking over a class, or picking up garbage. You can run on the playground in heels and sit at cafeteria tables, take money at the register, and perform so many tasks that some would consider "menial," and might not be in your job description. It doesn't matter. You have to do them, at least sometimes.

Just because you are a principal does not mean you are a prima donna. Maybe you can remember the first time as a school leader that you "helped out" with something outside of your job description. You probably never heard the end of that first time. It was like you had invented fire or something.

That's the secret here . . . small things go a very long way. It's priceless, and just one more thing that takes very little time, but reaps very large benefits. You obviously don't have time to man the phones all day, or become a full-time substitute, or drive the bus, but sometimes your staff and teachers are going to need help in a pinch, maybe only for a few minutes, and you will be standing there being a boss. Help them.

BE FUN

Being fun begins with *having* fun, and not taking yourself too seriously. You can be professional and appropriate and still have a smile on your face. Maybe you've had the experience of working with cranky people, possibly secretaries or any school leader, who are in a bad mood every day. Others may describe them and say, "Well, maybe they're just not morning people." In those two pivotal "PR" positions, if you're not a morning person by nature, you had better learn how to fake it, or start working with machines or widgets instead of people.

Sometimes this type of behavior is tolerated for far too long (think *The Devil Wears Prada*,[4] where the boss storms into the office and everyone ducks for cover), especially if this person is in a position of power. Maybe people think that it's easy for people who act happy and positive, thinking it is true to their nature, but maybe it isn't. The truth is that whether it's part of your nature or not, it's your job to make the choice to be happy and positive.

I'm sure you've seen the slogan "happiness is a choice." Some days it's easier than others to choose happiness, but when you are getting paid for something, you need to fake it until you make it. It sounds corny, but it's true. You don't get paid just to be competent, but to set the tone, especially when you are a leader or a boss.

Your personality can set the tone for the entire building, and even the research says that a positive work environment and being "happy" at work raises productivity. So there you have it . . . have fun and be fun, or at least be positive. This is demonstrated by the research behind the career of Tony Hsieh, the (now deceased) founder of the online retail company Zappos and author of *Delivering Happiness*.[5] If you love Zappos, it is probably due to how they treat their customers.

When you are working in a school setting, you can dress up for Halloween and other spirit days, do a staff skit or lip sync, or just walk around smiling. I can't tell you how many people comment on leaders walking around and smiling. It is the easiest thing in the world.

SHOW UP

"Showing up" is another vital part of focusing on your staff. Show up for things outside work, even if it's only for five minutes. You don't need to "hang out" with people. Just stop in—wakes, performances, athletic events, and so on. It bears repeating that a very small amount of time means a lot when you are the boss. You don't have to go to everything or you will go insane, but you need to choose a few things.

You could go into a basketball game for 10 minutes and 100 people will see you, and they will tell other people, and say, "Did you see the principal was here?" It validates everything the staff and students do, because it mirrors their daily hard work, their insanely exhausting daily hard work. You wouldn't be a leader if you hadn't already done it yourself, so you understand.

RESPECT THE CULTURE

Unless something is truly illegal, immoral, or just blatantly not working and it's all anyone is talking about, don't make any changes until you have been at your school for at least a year. This is leadership 101, but you would be surprised at how many leaders don't follow this rule, and it can affect the entire tenure of your leadership in a negative way. Even if you think you see something that needs to be changed, you might not have all the information. You probably will *not* have all the information, and even if you do, and the change is a good one, you won't have earned the respect and trust of your staff in order to do it.

You have to work side by side with them for a year first, maybe even longer. After a year, you can tweak things or introduce changes, but only with the help of a team and/or committee. It takes a long time to build trust, and relying on your teachers' experience and expertise is the smartest thing to do—for professional reasons, but also for personal ones. Many leaders are eager to jump in and prove themselves, when the exact opposite is what is needed most.

It can be challenging when you do have a committee and everyone is invited, and then the committee makes a decision and you find out later that someone is strongly opposed to it, but they never speak up. This can be difficult to swallow, but it happens. You have to gather as much information as possible, and listen to as many voices as will contribute, and make a final decision. That is your job, and sometimes it's challenging because no one will ever agree on one thing. This is something you can count on, and that's where your education and experience come in. You also need to be able to accept when not every single person is happy.

KNOW SERVICE AND SUPPORT STAFF

I think everyone knows this one already, and I mentioned it earlier, but it is worth repeating. The most important people are your secretary or administrative assistant, the maintenance crew, the mailman, UPS and delivery people, and so forth. Remember them at holidays with a small token or gift, and get to know them personally. Sometimes a box of quality chocolate in the maintenance room, or a basket of fresh fruit in the kitchen, is a welcome little surprise. This adds to the culture of the school, and everyone knows they are basically running the place, so give credit where credit is due.

GROW LEADERS

Maybe you are the type of leader that lets people take the ball and run with an idea, or lets them take charge of something you could easily do yourself. If so, you have probably found that some people are shocked by this or think it's a lazy way to lead. For all you leaders (and control freaks) out there, you know that nothing could be further from the truth. It is not easy. Giving people ownership and control is in fact very difficult, and sometimes things don't turn out exactly as you would have liked, but sometimes they actually turn out even better!

There is a famous leadership saying by Lao Tzu, "A leader is best when people barely know he exists, when his work is done, his aim fulfilled, they will say: we did it ourselves." You are all on the same team, and when you have a teacher presenting an idea at a staff meeting, people are really going to listen. You aren't the only person in the room with intelligence, ideas, and the ability to inspire others. This also helps your staff buy into initiatives, and come up with creative, wonderful ideas you could never have imagined. It is true that many minds are better than one.

You will never forget the school leader that believed in you, and gave you a chance to shine. You also won't forget the leader that was the first person to tell you that they thought *you* could be a school leader. All it takes is one person to plant the idea in your head, and give you the confidence to pursue it. You also don't forget the first time as a teacher that your principal asks you to chair a committee, present something to the entire faculty, or run with one of your ideas. A true leader grows and appreciates other leaders. You also can't lead your school forever, so someone needs to be waiting in the wings to take over.

LISTEN

When any new leader, teacher, or employee begins a new job, their gut instinct is to try to impress others with their experience, knowledge, and personality. This instinct couldn't be more wrong. The most difficult thing to do, especially when you are new, is simply to listen, but it's also the most necessary. If you walk into any faculty meeting, board room, classroom, parent conference, or office, and you begin by truly listening, people will walk away impressed by you, just because they have been heard.

This holds true for any conflict or complaint with anyone. If you take time to listen to what is going on, half of your issue will be rectified and the tension in the room will also dissipate. You have plenty of time to share your knowledge and impress people with your experience, but not until you listen. Additionally, when resolving conflict, there may be solutions, conclusions, and consequences that some involved parties aren't completely satisfied with, but if they have been listened to first, they will accept the conclusion much more readily.

NOTES

1. Laurel Schmidt, *Gardening in the Minefield: A Survival Guide for School Administrators* (Portsmouth: Heinemann, 2002), 24.
2. Margery Williams, *The Velveteen Rabbit* (London: Egmont Books, 2004).
3. Schmidt, *Gardening in the Minefield*.
4. David Frankel, *The Devil Wears Prada* (Fox 2000 Pictures, 2006).
5. Tony Hsieh, *Delivering Happiness: A Path to Profits, Passion, and Purpose* (New York: Grand Central Publishing, 2013).

Chapter 2

Self-Care

Most people who pursue school leadership positions are either crazy, or have a type A personality, or possibly a little bit of both. Who truly wants to be responsible for hundreds of people 24 hours a day, seven days a week? Perhaps people who have boundless energy, great determination, physical and emotional strength, curiosity, and grit. These types of people also might not be the best at taking care of themselves, and often burn out or put their physical and emotional well-being at risk. This section is for them.

SUPPORT NETWORK

It will be extremely valuable in your leadership world to have a support network of people that you love and trust, and can be completely honest with. Some refer to this as their Inner Circle, or IC. At every job, you should seek out some obvious people to be in this group, as well as some not so obvious ones. You cannot carry the weight of the world on your shoulders. For most, it will be even more important and necessary to have an IC at home—your spouse, partner, children, parents, siblings, and friends.

You might also be able to have an IC at work, which could include anyone from your administrative assistant to the maintenance staff. You'll learn quickly who you can trust. It's probably safest at work to never be 100 percent transparent or share truly confidential information, because you could be burned or betrayed. Everyone knows how salacious commentary from the school leader is, but nonetheless, it can be helpful to talk to a select few. Sometimes even frustrations or challenges can be shared with others in a helpful way.

Most school leaders wish to behave ultraprofessionally at work, but experience indicates that this could also result in having a team that is not truly on the same page with you. If the institution is experiencing financial issues, or other internal or external challenges, sharing a general feeling without specifics will help explain actions and allow initiatives to be more readily accepted and supported. You don't have to be negative and gossipy in order for others to be on the same page with you.

At home, maybe your partner and children hear it all, and since they are probably not even listening sometimes, possibly don't remember much of what you say, and would never repeat it to anyone, it can be a safe place to fall. Having a home IC is crucial to stable mental health, and also should never be taken advantage of. It's important to know how much to share, when to share, and when to stop and leave some of it behind at school. You can't take advantage of your home IC or they will burn out, too, mostly because they care about you and don't want to see you stressed.

TAKE CARE OF YOUR OWN HEALTH

This is so important, and most people are not as good at it as they could or should be, but you have to keep working on it. Most school leaders probably think that a good day is when you get to go to the bathroom, or that a good day is when you get to eat. You would think school leaders would be emaciated for how many days they never eat at work, but you always make up for it when you get home. There are only so many hours in a day, and they run out pretty quickly when you are so busy, but you have to walk away, go home, go for a run, walk around a store, have a glass of wine, or do anything to quiet your mind.

Sometimes you have to shut your door, even though you don't want people to think you don't have an open door policy, even if it's only for five minutes to breathe. Shut your door. Walk out the door. Leave early. Come in late. Being a school leader, or any type of leader, is hard work. You need to take care of *you*. Wherever you go, you need to be *on*. If you don't sleep well one night, that's ok, because you will probably sleep well the next night. You need to catch up on your sleep, even if it's only for one day a week, and even if it's only for eight hours that one day.

Everyone has their own strategies to restore their balance and mental health. Maybe you enjoy cleaning, running, yoga, puttering, shopping, interior design, spending time with family, baking, cooking, doing laundry, reading, watching movies or sports. You need to find what is right for you and make sure you take time to do it. Take care of you, or you can't do this type of job.

IMAGE/APPEARANCE

For those very rare occasions you may attempt to run into a grocery store, hoping not to see anyone, wearing running clothes, a baseball hat and no makeup, you will always see someone. It's not that you have to be perfect all the time, but in some weird way, you have to look decent. Not immaculate, but not like you just rolled out of bed. This possibly contradicts the second chapter advice to Be Real, but it is the reality of leadership.

This has more to do with how *you* feel when you run into people; it probably doesn't matter as much to them. If they aren't your favorite online sites already, two to check out are Zappos and Amazon, and now you can even buy groceries online and have them delivered. It can also be helpful to get your clothes ready the night before or, if you're feeling really ambitious, get five outfits ready for the entire week. Hopefully you will actually "feel" like wearing all five when the day comes, depending on meetings that day, as well as how much walking is involved if you are a woman in heels.

You are seen as a role model as a school principal, and you want to be professional, but you can also try to look interesting. In an all girls' high school or an elementary school, you can wear colored tights, and some glittery pink or red shoes, even with a black suit or dress, are much appreciated. A little sparkle goes a long way. For male leaders, an interesting collection of socks or ties can be endearing, and if you are gender neutral, you will also find a "look" that works for you. You want to be professional while still exhibiting your personality in some way. Remember: you are working with children!

STRESS

The category of stress is just as important as taking care of your own health. They go hand in hand, and if you don't take care of yourself and learn to navigate the constant stress of leading a school building or district, it can eat you up and spit you out. The one thing you can count on every hour, every day in a school, is stress. This can most likely be said about any job where you are leading and managing people; then add teachers, students, parents, and an involved community, and it can become a powder keg.

You can count on that. You will never have a typical day where you can accomplish what you want to, or where everything will go as planned. That's the exciting and interesting part of the job, and also the part that can take you down with it. Many brand new administrators fizzle out fast when they take everything in, and take everything personally, and react to everything in a heightened way. Besides causing physical damage to your body, the way you handle stress can also affect the tone in the building.

There will be stress. Every day. Maybe an elementary student will call you out on the playground because someone has just drawn a huge "wiener and two balls" in chalk on the basketball court. Perhaps the fire alarm will go off without warning or you will smell smoke coming from the science lab wing, or an unexpected parent will show up at your door or march right into your office because they are angry, hurt, or upset, or because someone did not get back to them in a timely manner.

Most likely you had a teacher post something political or inappropriate on Facebook and received an email about it, or one of your high school students acted inappropriately on TikTok, or at a basketball game. Maybe a teacher swore in their classroom. All day long. The trick is to put each situation in perspective. Look at the big picture. Smile. Take a breath. In the grand scheme of things, it will all be ok. Even when a child gets sick, or loses a parent, or has a bad injury or surgery, you will be able to find the right words, and the right supports that they need. You will be enough.

If you have good intentions, and are able to admit when you've made a mistake, or your teacher acted inappropriately, or you missed a phone call or an email, you will be ok. Then you will leave it at work, and go home, and try not to check your email after a certain hour. You will enjoy your time at home, whether you have a family or not, and you will take a break, get some sleep, and get ready to begin all over again the next day.

The other important part of handling stress is to realize that you don't have to handle everything alone. Many new administrators get into the weeds and try to address every single little thing themselves. Of course every single little thing will come to you if you are tuned in and have your finger on the "daily pulse," but every experienced school leader knows that you don't actually have to be the person who takes care of everything.

You undoubtedly will have wonderful assistants, teachers, and staff working with you that are ready, willing, and able to take care of things if you ask them. Always give them timelines and target dates, and have them get back to you when situations are addressed. Then all you have to do is be grateful. You will also soon learn which things need the school leader to take care of. Experience teaches you that.

FAMILY FIRST

Whether you believe it or not, you need to make it clear to your staff that their families come first. Some may disagree with this and say your job comes first, but if you don't value their families, then they can't value their jobs. Tell your staff this on the first day, and you will never have anyone take advantage of your understanding of their family obligations. Just like with everything else, if you let them leave work five minutes early for a dance recital or come in 10 minutes late because they took their child to their first day of kindergarten, they'll make it up in their work a million times over.

If you're comfortable, it's also nice to include your own family, and bring them to school functions with you. This sets the tone and makes it a lot easier when you are spending time away from home. It also shows that you value your own family as much as you are valuing the family of your teachers and staff.

They will not only come in body, mind, and spirit, but give financially to fundraisers when able to do so. It's another way to show you value your school community. Encourage everyone to bring their children and families to events, too. Hopefully this will happen naturally. All of your work lives and home lives will blend together, and since you spend the majority of your life at work, this is a very positive thing.

Chapter 3

Character

Many of the previous chapters have touched on something that is at the core of being a good leader, role model, and facilitator of all things that support and care for our children: good character. No school leader is perfect, but everyone knows when they witness good character, whether it is found in the head of our parent group or the president of our country. Everyone can benefit from focusing on what it means to have good character and to be a good person at our core. You simply cannot have questionable character and lead a school well. The areas specified here are simply the basics of what that can mean.

DON'T GOSSIP

I mean, everyone is human, and may certainly spill "our truth" about people and situations at home, and it's a definite plus if your IC never repeats anything you have shared, but even if you think you have someone at work you can trust with your personal thoughts, think twice. It's just not worth it, and neither is gossip. Maybe you have worked with leadership teams who treat gossiping or talking negatively about someone like a sport, but just don't do it. Period.

This sometimes leads groups to not like you as much because you won't join in, but anyone of true value won't care if you don't gossip or join in, and anyone of true value won't do it in the first place. Besides it being unkind and unprofessional, it's also just bad business.

Worlds collide in so many ways and you never know if the person you gossiped about will be the one person you really need to help you with something. Seriously, who cares about gossip anyway? You can get all your guilty pleasures binge-watching Netflix, so who needs more than that? None of us are perfect, and everyone will probably roll their eyes at some point, or even join in for a second, or seem to condone it by not saying anything. You will always regret it, feel bad about it, and usually have it bite you in the bum. Don't gossip.

HAVE FAITH

Have faith in something or someone. Even if your someone happens to be Jesus Christ, Buddha, Allah, or Krishna, you would be surprised how both public and private schools will allow you to share that faith at appropriate times. Of course, first you need to read the room, but in general you can't go wrong with sharing your faith. Some schools may have specific policies banning any allusion to a specific faith, so you have to familiarize yourself with them before moving forward. Even if your faith practice is different from that of your teachers and staff, they will be heartened and comforted that you rely on a higher power to do your work.

SAY THANK YOU

Say "thank you" to everyone who deserves it and even to those who don't. This is a big part of your job. When you say "thank you" and truly mean it, people only want to do more. Everyone in the world wants to be acknowledged and appreciated. It is a basic human need. Most people are also somewhat insecure, even the ones who seem the most secure. A quick email or handwritten note goes a long way.

Email is fine, but you can also purchase small note cards almost anywhere for about $10 for 100. They are small and gorgeous and can be mailed, or put in someone's school mailbox. For most events, you may be the person doing a lot of the work, or maybe your assistant will be in the weeds doing the bulk of the work. Still, it is your job to show appreciation and be grateful for the work done in the trenches.

At Christmas, you are going to receive gifts whether you like it or not, and it's a nice idea to sit in your office for an hour or so on the last day and write out your thank-you notes so it doesn't take up your holiday. You might prefer it if you didn't receive any gifts, because how many scented candles can you actually use?

People will give you gifts because of your position, or maybe because they truly appreciate you. Sometimes faculty decide that in lieu of gifts, everyone donates whatever amount of money they can, and you then donate it to some needy families in your school or community, or a charity of your choice. This idea can come from you.

It can be overwhelming (to say the least) being given so much love in return. When you give of yourself for the sake of others, you don't really expect or want all that you will receive in return, so you need to know that if you follow this advice, you are going to be loved and appreciated so much you might have to leave town for a while, at least once a year.

Sometimes school leaders are in charge of coordinating the graduation ceremony for your school, and for anyone that has done this, you know how much work and attention to detail it takes. Even though you may have earned several degrees and possibly even have a PhD, you may sometimes feel like an event planner, but that's also part of the job.

After big, important events that your entire school is involved in, it's nice to send out individual thank-you notes to everyone, even though you may have basically planned most of the event. Once you get over this fact, and you see how far your gratitude goes, you will want to thank everyone!

This may seem ridiculous, but it truly pays off in the long run. Instead of just using the thank-you notes to specifically mention what they did for the event, you can also use this note to thank them for whatever makes them special in the school. It can even become an annual tradition. When you walk into offices or classrooms and see your note hanging on a bulletin board, you will understand how important it is.

SEE THE GOOD

See the good in people and they will be even better! Everyone in a position of authority has enough experience to nitpick and criticize, and constructive criticism has its place, but in general, the more positive you are, the more you will receive back in all areas from your employees. This structure is what is sometimes called an "enabling school structure."

This type of structure will help teachers and staff believe in the very best of themselves, and in turn they will do their best work for their students. This type of structure fosters collaboration, innovation, and trust among its members, and guides problem solving instead of punishing failure and focusing on the negative.

Many teachers have experienced a leadership model where negatives are highlighted and pointed out, and, for example, leaders look at their watches if you are a minute late on a snowy day. We have all been there, and hopefully we have also experienced the loving and understanding look on their face that time we were late when there was a last-minute diaper to change or an accident on the highway. It feels better to be supported and understood, and can propel you to make up for being late in other ways.

PART II

Head: Book Smart, Street Smart

The "head" part of school leadership is the part that most graduate and doctorate programs focus on and stress. It is a very important part, and honestly, if you can't do the job, and follow school law, and tend to the nuts and bolts of the position in an organized way, then you will not be successful as a leader. It's as simple as that. The central thesis of this book is that "head" alone is just not enough, and for anyone that has worked with a school leader that is excellent in this area, but lacks the heart of leadership, you know exactly what that means.

Chapter 4

Book Smart

These areas are the "bread and butter" of a good school leader. Once you earn your leadership degree, complete your administrative internship, and get your first job as an assistant principal or principal, staying current with research, trends, and strategies that will help your school community is the most useful thing you can do. In addition, when it comes to informing and supporting your students, teachers, and parents, you need a well-researched, continually updated "bag of tricks." It also takes the onus off what you may "think" to be true, and it's easier to use and get support for, since it's vetted by experts other than yourself.

RESEARCH AND TRENDS

As you grow in experience as a school leader, this area will grow in its value to you and to the school communities you serve. Anyone who has written a research paper or journal article, or completed a full doctoral dissertation, understands that the importance of research cannot be devalued. People in your school community may disagree with you or your philosophies, but it's difficult to poo-poo (a technical term) valid, well-conducted research. Everyone conducts quick Google searches when they are looking for support or information, but nothing can take the place of scholarly, peer-reviewed research, and using it to support ideas and initiatives is invaluable.

One of the most important research areas you will encounter if you are an elementary school principal is the subject of early intervention. Programs like Head Start and early interventions in such areas as speech, physical therapy, occupational therapy are invaluable. Also, programs like AIS (Academic Intervention Services) and RTI (Response to Intervention) are also research-based and proven to show academic gains, especially when students are not responding to the typical methods of teaching.

Other areas where it's vital to review, understand, and share research with your community include mental health, developmental disabilities, learning disabilities (including ADHD, ASD, ODD, OCD), and appropriate interventions and supports. ADHD is now more accurately referred to as "variable attention stimulus trait" or VAST. Hopefully every college program includes an entire course on both exceptional and special education. It seems that the most difficult part of addressing deficits of any kind is the initial diagnosis. It's very challenging for parents and children to take that first step of testing and assessment for many reasons, one of them being that they are afraid a label will follow and limit their child. Honestly, this is rarely the case, but for those of you who have children with any type of learning or behavioral disability or obstacle, it is understandable where it comes from. Empathy and support are crucial here.

It's also important to understand topics such as diversity and equity, gaming and media use, and bullying. In the area of gaming and media use, for example, as well as gender differences in adolescence, one well-known expert is Dr. Leonard Sax. (He is also a worthwhile speaker, as he often shares his research and insight regarding these topics.) There is a solidly research-based antibullying program called Olewus, in which every single person in a district is trained, from the bus drivers to the superintendent.

It is very powerful to share with high school boys that the recommended time spent playing video games is 40 minutes per weekday, and an hour and a half on weekends. They may get extremely defensive at first, but it opens up a conversation. Even more powerful is the discussion involving games with a so-called moral inversion, like the *Grand Theft Auto* series. Research conducted by Dr. Sax has found that games that promote moral inversions in thinking can actually change adolescents' personality traits, and cause them to be less empathetic and kind.[1]

One bit of advice for school leaders who have been in the job for more than a few years is to expand their toolbox in this area. Most leaders begin their teaching and leadership journeys with our "Ms. or Mr. America" platforms, and that's great, but research changes and is updated, and there are new buzzwords and research results, and you need to stay current. If you have some research you share with teachers or parents that is powerful and effective, remember to update and/or revise your "shtick" every year. Every educator has witnessed both teachers and school leaders who are singing the same song for their entire career, or recommending the same book. This is not good. Stay up on research!

BRAIN RESEARCH

Beginning in 2000, advances in brain imaging began to teach us things about the brain, specifically the adolescent brain, that one could have only guessed at before. One of the most important findings, and one that is important to share with parents and teachers, pertains to the subject of brain maturation. This research cited by Lawrence Steinberg helps explain that the development of advanced abilities in adolescents may not be complete until individuals reach their mid-20s.[2]

Understanding this about their development does not mean that adolescents are given a pass for bad decision-making or behavior. This is not about making excuses for them, but trying to better understand why otherwise responsible young adults sometimes make bad decisions. This can help them forgive themselves and move on, and hopefully not make the same choice twice. Anyone with an adolescent-aged child, or anyone who works with them, understands why this insight is so important.

This also has important ramifications for understanding adolescent behavior and decision-making, as well as the actions parents and important people in adolescents' lives need to take when they make a mistake or a bad decision. For example, brain scans show that teenagers will make a different decision in the presence of peers than when alone. The actual chemistry of the brain is changed! This affects decisions about everything from driving to peer pressure. These findings support laws that require teenagers that don't drive with peers in their cars until a certain age, and also explain why they sometimes need constant discussions about making the right decision, especially when they are with their friends.

STUDY SKILLS

This topic is extremely powerful for educators, parents and school leaders, and possibly more important than has often been recognized. Hopefully some of you have been fortunate to have honed many study skills your parents and teachers taught you, developing what works over the years, as many good students do. Some students are just spinning their wheels and wasting time, when a few simple strategies can give them more "bang for their buck." These strategies are also based on 100 years of research.

There are many compilations of study strategy books on the market, and one extremely helpful one is Benedict Carrey's *How We Learn*.[3] These strategies can provide help to parents, struggling students, and teachers who can't seem to reach them with advice on how to be successful. Many study strategies can also be applied to how students get themselves organized, not only for school, but also for life.

It can be beneficial to hold book studies with teachers using this kind of book, so teachers can use the same terminology as their students, and then they aren't teaching strategies that contradict each other. It's doable to have teachers read perhaps a chapter per month, and then meet in small groups, or even remotely, to discuss. They can then roll out a plan including specific strategies that will be shared with students. Some schools actually build study skills training into their regular professional development for teachers, and also offer classes for students so everyone in the school has the same strategies.

If your school doesn't already have one, it's a great idea to have someone teach a study skills class to every student. Maybe you could even offer to do this yourself, as it's a great way to meet and spend time with your students. It can be a "boot camp" and last a week or two, or can be woven into the calendar year.

The basic strategy of "spacing out studying"[4] can save time and increase test scores, and no parent or teacher can argue with that. If for example, students study 15 minutes a night for four nights instead of two hours the night before an exam, it will give their brains time to form permanent synapses and connections, as well as saving them time. Giving students and parents strategies gives them power and support.

Another proven strategy that may seem old-school is "writing things down," which can be more effective and powerful than looking on your phone calendar, or on your school website. Every time you put pen to paper, it activates something in the base of your brain called the "reticular activating system," or the "RAS" and it goes into our long term memory in a deeper way than via other methods. This is perhaps why many of us still use some version of a paper datebook or calendar to stay organized.

If students are struggling with reading, which they seem to be more than ever since COVID, a good resource is Cris Tovani's original book, *I Read It but I Don't Get It*,[5] and her three follow-up books. She advises that matching a student with a book that they will like, as well as one that is appropriate, is important.

Another very useful tool is the YouTube videos put out by Thomas Frank[6] about study skills and other helpful life skills that students need and appreciate. These videos include topics like how to build discipline and healthy habits, how to set up a study space in your home, habits of organized people, and a recently released video for anyone feeling behind in life. Students appreciate hearing someone, sometimes someone other than their teacher or parent, telling them how to organize their lives, while at the same time reassuring them that they are normal, and fine.

GRIT, ETC.

Another important area that you can share with students and parents, and one that is also based on years of brain research, is the concept of "grit." Many students grow up thinking that they are one type of student, which is either successful, average, or poor. This sadly also defines who they are since they spend so much of their time in school, which predominantly measures one type of learning, one type of intelligence.

Sharing the work of Angela Duckworth on the topic of "grit,"[7] and Carol Dweck's[8] ideas about having a "growth mindset" shows that the mere teaching of different brain capabilities to students increases their academic success. Learning ability is not fixed, and students and parents need to be aware of this research. Since Duckworth's research, there has been pushback claiming that this concept might not be helpful for students on the autism spectrum, or possibly those from lower socioeconomic backgrounds, but teachers can individualize supports and strategies for each student.

Teachers and coaches can introduce this concept by showing Ted Talks about "grit" that Angela Duckworth has presented, then having their students complete either the short or long version of the "grit" scale, which will give them a score of 1–5, 5 being the "grittiest." This is followed by a discussion demonstrating that "grit" is a skill that can be grown, and is not fixed. This is very powerful for students who don't feel successful at school. Coupled with study skills and opportunities to have their learning differentiated, it can change the trajectory of their success in school, and most importantly, how they feel about being in school.

This goes hand in hand with the work that has been done on the qualities of self-regulation and delayed gratification as being important in the world of academics and decision-making. Not everyone realizes that delayed gratification is so predictive of future success. Remember Mischel's Stanford Marshmallow experiment?[9] In this classic study, children that were able to resist eating a marshmallow were awarded two, showing a strong correlation between delaying gratification and success in life.

PROFESSIONAL DEVELOPMENT

Many schools have budgeting monies for professional development and teacher training, but unfortunately, some do not. There will hopefully always be teachers who will seek it out on their own, and in some states and public schools, there are annual requirement hours to maintain teaching certification. Wherever you are and whatever the budget, offering professional development several times a year is vital for keeping up on instructional topics and trends, and even more importantly, for team building.

Some of the best workdays are times when you and your teachers and staff get together for things that bond you together as professionals and friends. This could include engaging in a drumming seminar, diversity training and awareness, a retreat or time off campus, a day of bowling, guest speakers on mental health, student presentations, and almost anything creative you can think of.

One really good idea, especially in our current educational climate, is to plan and execute a mental health and wellness day. Potential stations might be yoga, essential oil mixing, prayer and meditation, ultimate Frisbee football, and cupcake decorating (and eating), as well as curriculum mapping or revision, individual and departmental goal-setting, and brainstorming for student activities and events.

Even with the fun team building days, you need to provide some content. It's also important to canvas faculty and staff and see what they want, and what their feedback is. No matter how wonderful the professional development is, there will always be naysayers, and the number of teachers who dislike what is planned will decrease if it comes from their ideas and needs.

NOTES

1. Leonard Sax, *Boys Adrift: The Five Factors Driving the Growing Epidemic of Unmotivated Boys and Underachieving Young Men* (New York: Little, Brown and Company, 2016).

2. Lawrence Steinberg, *Adolescence* (New York: McGraw Hill, 2023).

3. Benedict Carey, *How We Learn: The Surprising Truth about When, Where, and Why It Happens* (New York: Random House, 2015).

4. Ibid.

5. Chris Tovani, *I Read It but I Don't Get It: Comprehension Strategies for Adolescent Readers* (Portland: Stenhouse Publishers, 2000).

6. Thomas Frank, "13 Essential, Science-Backed Study Tips" (YouTube video, 2019), https://www.youtube.com/watch?v=Bxv9lf5HjZM.

7. Angela Duckworth, *Grit: The Power of Passion and Perseverance* (New York: Scribner, 2016).

8. Carol Dweck, *Mindset: The New Psychology of Success* (New York: Ballantine Books, 2006).

9. Walter Mischel, *The Marshmallow Test: Why Self-Control Is the Engine of Success* (New York: Little, Brown and Company, 2015).

Chapter 5

Street Smart

There are so many things that you can do "right" as a school leader, but there is nothing like experience to make you the best leader you can be. The "tincture of time" will improve your skills in all areas, but only if you are paying attention. Some school leaders never master the art of listening, and spending time learning, because their egos get in the way. They spend every year like their very first year, and never learn or improve. Once you gain experience, you will be able to draw on it and apply your newfound "street smarts" to do even better. "Every crisis is an opportunity for creativity, and sometimes even greatness" (anonymous).

DO THE JOB

Hopefully this is obvious, and not really what this book is all about. You can be the kindest leader in the world, but that will all fade away if you are not competent. The behaviors this book is focusing on are the things that can set you apart and make your leadership effective and special. Doing the job is a whole other category that could be described in every area of leadership that exists.

You need to know the work, the regulations, the legalities, the lingo, the trends, and, if you work in a union shop, the contract. You need to know how to document everything, and to do what is best for staff, students, and your school in every way possible. You need to follow up on every tiny thing, and keep detailed records. This is time-consuming and stressful, but find a system that works for you and follow up. Your system may include different types of spiral notebooks and files, both digital and analog for different types of notes and follow-ups. Keep organizing as you go, and write everything down so you can prioritize things daily.

EXPERIENCE

Everyone has to start new at some point, but before you get your first job as a school leader, you will hopefully have experienced an administrative internship or have held the position of department chair leader, or more importantly, assistant or vice principal. There is no shortcut to gaining experience in every single area, and there are hundreds of situations that you will encounter in your first year as a school leader. The worst thing a new leader can do is to lead with ego. Perhaps you are coming from a different grade level, or maybe you are newly certified and are moving from a different field altogether, which will bring its own challenges.

If you listen and take notes, and take a step back before you make decisions, you are still going to make mistakes—that is a given—but hopefully you will not make the same mistake twice. After a year or two, you will have experienced almost every possible challenge as a school leader, but even years into it, sometimes something will come up, and you will think, "Wow, that's a new one." If you don't have the relevant experience, ask someone who does and rely on the experts who have been through it before.

Nothing is worse than witnessing a brand-new leader make decisions based on their gut, and their gut alone, which usually have to be retracted or revised because the decision is just wrong, and usually not best for students. It's fine not to have experience, but it's not fine to act like you know it all.

Also, after years of experience, don't be afraid to be open to trying something different. Your legacy doesn't have to be based on Shirley Jackson's short story, "The Lottery,"[1] where things are done the same way all the time because that's the way they have always been done. If you are not familiar with the annual stoning that takes place in her story, it's a worthwhile read.

BE PREPARED

"Luck favors the prepared" is a school leader's motto to live by. People will believe that you are good at many things, including public speaking, remembering names, and commenting on initiatives, regulations, school law, and so forth, based on the simple fact that you were prepared, and did your homework. For every meeting, event, or discussion, do just a little bit of background work and preparation. It's safe to say that you will be ahead of most people that are participating.

Again, it's the easiest thing to do if you come up with a system for yourself, and it will make you feel so much more confident and comfortable if you go into every situation armed with background information, names, and the like.

One way to do this is what is referred to as the "pile method," which simply means making a pile of information you will need for every day, and looking over it briefly, putting each topic on the bottom of the pile as you go. If you don't have a hard copy, write a note on where this information exists—maybe in an email, a Google doc, an online search, or the notes section of your phone. Being prepared takes very little time, and reaps large benefits.

FOLLOW UP

This falls under the category of "do the job," but it's important enough to single out and reiterate. Leaders who don't follow up are disrespectful to others. If you get an email, phone call, or question from someone when you are walking the halls (remember the little pad of paper you should carry around), jot it down, find an answer, and get back to the person. Getting back to them is sometimes more important than the answer itself, but it's better if you have one.

If you don't, tell them that and try to figure it out, or give them the resource or contact person to do it. Many school leaders believe that they need to figure everything out on their own, but once you finally start cutting out the middleman (or -woman) you will start saving time.

Often teachers and parents will say, "I know this is trivial and small and stupid to bring to you . . . but . . . ." Even though some things do seem trivial and small, they are sometimes indicative of bigger, festering issues. Some principals make a practice of saying things are not a priority, so they don't follow up promptly, or sometimes at all. That is a mistake, and also a missed opportunity.

In addition, sometimes a parent or staff member just needs a little attention, a little TLC, and then they are happy and feel comfortable with you. Sometimes you never hear from them again and they become silent cheerleaders or allies for you, which you need! Once in a while, they are people that become needier and needier all the time. That's ok, too. You just need to create some boundaries around your time with them. Don't run from them . . . all the energy they are putting into talking to you will soon be directed towards you, so make sure it's positive. Give them your time. Sometimes giving time saves time.

There seems to exist a phenomenon around holidays or the end of the school year. If you are trying to get out of work to enjoy your holiday or leave on vacation, always plan on dealing with a crisis at the last minute. Clear your afternoon schedule on these days. It may be difficult to understand why parents and staff like to bring big issues to you on the last day before Christmas, but maybe they feel they can't begin their holiday until they unload their problems on someone else, and that someone else will most likely be you.

ORGANIZATION

Find a system that works for you, and use it all the time. This system should include everything, for example, when people are having surgeries, their birthdays, and also your own personal appointments.

As mentioned in a previous chapter, it can be incredibly useful to write things down. It seems "old school," but if you write things down, and look at your datebook or calendar frequently, you will actually be able to visualize it even when you are not looking at it. The reticular activating system in the base of your brain will do part of the work of remembering for you, and everyone needs a little help.

Once you find a datebook you like, many companies offer inexpensive paper insert refills every year. A digital calendar is also a great supplement, since you don't have to rewrite birthdays or special days.

STAY CALM

In all things stay calm. Whether a student is hurt, or you smell gas, or a crazy parent storms the office, or the fire alarm goes off unexpectedly . . . your sense of calm will be contagious, and everyone will model what you are portraying. Even if you don't respond perfectly and remember every detail, that's ok. If you remain calm and ask for help, everything will be fine.

Your preparedness will also come in handy in a real crisis. Conduct emergency drills of every kind, including fire, shelter in place, full evacuation, and evacuation to alternate sites; practice whatever your regulations require you to do, and then do more. Assemble a crisis response team in your school that includes administration, your nurse, school counselors, and whoever will be able to add valuable input. Have your local police visit the school to practice such things as drills with real officers and drug-sniffing dogs, and make sure they have a key to your school and a map of it.

Some school leaders are reluctant to practice drills at times of the day that may prove challenging, but don't shy away from these times—lunch, passing times, dismissal times. You cannot predict when something may happen, and everyone will look to you for directions and guidance, so be up on regulations, and practice and prepare for whatever you can. The more prepared people are, the better they will respond in a crisis, so drill regularly, so procedures will come naturally in case of a real emergency.

REVIEW EACH DAY

It's pretty universal for all leaders, and people, to review each day, unless (God willing) you are too bone tired to do so. This should be a positive process, and it usually is, but you may also end up remembering the one person whose name you forgot, or the one person you forgot to thank, or whom you may have slighted because you were talking to a few other people at the same time. Sometimes you will feel the burn that comes when you were betrayed, or everyone didn't agree on a decision that you made.

If you committed a faux pas, don't get out of bed and send an email or text, or make a phone call to try to make it right, because usually the other person didn't even notice. It helps to keep a pad of paper near your bed, to jot down a note so you can fix it the next day. Then, you have to let it go and remember the good parts of the day and the things you did right. It bears repeating: you don't have to be perfect to every person and in every situation. Learn to laugh at yourself, let go, and move on. This is something most people continue to work on.

When you make a decision that not everyone is happy with—and this will happen with every decision you make—take time in the following days to talk privately to anyone who you know was opposed to it. Hear them out, and explain the decision further if you think you need to. Everyone won't always agree with your decisions, but if they are for the good of the school, and you give them a chance to voice their opinion, they will respect you for it, and ultimately, they will be ok with it.

SLEEP ON IT

Hopefully you have experienced that feeling that comes when you have a great brainstorm meeting with a small group and everyone has great ideas, and even when you think that yours may be pretty good, everyone listens and discusses them, and then someone decides you should all "sleep on it" and come back the next day . . . and then the ideas are even better!

No matter what the problem or issue is, sleep on it, run on it, take a shower with it . . . it always gets better . . . always, always, always. Take away your ego . . . no ego . . . and it will lead to success. Every leader has to have some kind of a healthy ego to be a school leader, but the older and more experienced you get, you realize that you don't have anything to prove by puffing up your chest. New leaders don't always realize when they need to take a step back. First instincts always get better with a little sleep. If no one suggests "sleeping on it," be that person.

NOTE

1. Shirley Jackson, *The Lottery and Other Stories* (New York: Farrar, Straus, and Giroux, 1949).

PART III

Head and Heart: Teachers, Students, Everyone

Some challenges and issues can be handled primarily with the heart, and a love of education and doing what is best for children, while some things are best navigated by good old-fashioned education and experience. Finally, there are those things that require a balanced combination of both.

Chapter 6

Teachers

Teachers are an invaluable resource for school leaders. Some leaders believe that once they have good teachers in place, their job is done, and they can focus on the other things that come their way every day. Nothing could be further from the truth. Teachers want freedom and autonomy, but they also need daily support, feedback, resources, and for leaders to value their input. They are your biggest asset, but can also turn into your biggest problem if you don't "feed" them.

STAFF AND COMMITTEE MEETINGS

There are many different ways that you can organize staff and committee meetings. Some school leaders like to schedule and hold monthly faculty meetings, as well as monthly meetings in areas such as technology, diversity, development, student issues, discipline, and professional development. Other leaders shy away from regular meetings and hold the bare minimum. It seems that something somewhere in the middle makes most people happy, since it's not too much of a time commitment, but things get done when there is a regularly scheduled meeting on the calendar.

In regards to what happens at these meetings, it's important that you have an agenda that others can contribute to, that everyone gets a chance to talk, and that you set talking rules and time limits. There also needs to be a limit to the length of the meeting so everyone can plan on a beginning and an end. The most important thing is that there needs to be food. Food can be provided in many ways; the best is probably to appoint a "snack captain" of some sort that is assigned to bring the food for each meeting. If this is the case, a small budget should be provided.

Another way to ensure that food is provided is to hire your cafeteria staff to provide a small snack and drink. (They usually can do this for a nominal fee.) Food makes people enjoy the meeting more, and tides them over until dinner, so they aren't cranky. As a school leader, it is your job to keep things focused and moving in the right direction, but if you become just a "talking head" sharing information and upcoming calendar dates, your people will walk away feeling the meeting was a waste of time. You can also use this time to organize your teachers and staff into small groups to work on initiatives and projects.

HIRING AND RETENTION

Of course you want to hire the best people, and of course you want them to stick around. That way they can get better each year, you can develop relationships with them, and you don't have to constantly look for new wonderful people. Principals and their teams sometimes have different philosophies on how to attract and hire the best teachers, but hopefully they all can agree on the basics. First, cast a wide net by asking your own teachers to spread the word.

Next, it's important to use all the forms of social media and networking websites that you have at your disposal, along with college recruitment pages, and even good old-fashioned newspaper ads (which will also be available online). Yes, some people still look for jobs in the newspaper and on sites like Indeed. Some of these ads cost more than others, so expect to pay a few hundred dollars.

There are various ways to collect resumes, but it's effective if they can come directly to you, to be reviewed by you. You can also make them available to your assistant principal, a department chair, and the director of guidance or another staff member that works closely with the teachers. Once everyone chooses their top ten, then try to narrow it down further, and ask your administrative assistant to schedule interviews by calling them personally. Usually you will get about 80 percent of your candidates to schedule an interview time.

Even if the candidate does not come in, the time your administrative assistant spends speaking to them can help the school's reputation. Even in a public school, where enrollment numbers do not rule the day, your reputation is projected in every call made on your behalf. It's important that you observe some of these interactions, and if it's not happening in a positive and attentive way, speak to the person making the calls, or even make the calls yourself. This takes some extra time, but says a lot about your leadership. Some people may disagree and think that the impression an outside applicant has of you, your team, and your school doesn't matter, but it does. It all matters.

Once interviews are scheduled, it's important that you meet with your interview team ahead of time and agree on what your procedures will be.

You should each develop specific questions, possibly three or so each. Taken together, the questions should cover all important areas. All the same questions should be asked of every candidate for equity, and notes should be taken in case there is a misremembering later on.

It's extremely important that every person that comes into your school feels welcomed and comfortable, whether they are offered the job or not. Be prepared to let the staff know who they are when they are waiting, to offer them water and coffee, or another appropriate refreshment. Sometimes the information gleaned from your staff while the candidate is waiting, or the "interview before the interview," speaks volumes. It also makes your staff feel that their feedback matters, because it does. They may see something the committee does not: for example, if the candidate is rude or on their phone the entire time they are waiting, that may indicate something.

Sometimes people value experience in a teacher over everything else, but it's also true that taking a chance on someone who is interviewing for their very first teaching job can be worth the risk. You will know a good fit for your school's culture when you meet them, so don't be afraid to go with your gut, and the collective consensus of the committee. The person who is the right fit will soon catch up with experience if they are open and willing to learn. Plus, sometimes it's a positive that they are not already "set in their ways" as to how things have been done in the past.

If you are interviewing for the high school level, you of course want your representative from that department to feel that they want to work with the person, as they may be spending more time with them than you. You never want to hire someone that they don't feel comfortable with, and you might have to give up your first choice.

In regards to having teachers come in and teach a lesson, there are many different opinions. You definitely want to check all their references and have your two or three finalists come at least a second time, but teaching an actual lesson or mini lesson is up to you. Sometimes you may need this additional step to make a sound decision, and sometimes it's not necessary. Sometimes it's just awkward for all parties involved, having students present, or having teachers "act like students."

Some principals may disagree on this, but the way you reject, or do not choose, candidates, is also very important, and a reflection on you. A phone call or an individual note goes a long way to help someone in their search for the right position—even if it's not with you. They will remember *how* they were "rejected," and for anyone who values working in education, this is important for the good of the profession. Plus, everyone can relate to how good a positive rejection feels.

Once you hire a good teacher, your work is only just beginning. Most schools have formal mentoring programs that are actually mandated by their state regulations, and even for those who do, the formal mentoring of a teacher is always supplemented by people in their school that become their informal mentors. That includes the principal.

The first thing you can do to ensure that good teachers are happy and stay with you, is a strong, comprehensive orientation program that takes place in the summer, before they enter the school. This should cover all the necessary legal areas, such as abuse training, but also everything specific to your school and district. A formal hard copy of all materials is helpful, as all this information can be overwhelming for them, and it's good for them to have something to look back on. In bigger districts, there is usually formal training as a group, and also building-level specifics.

You will want them to have everything they need to feel comfortable, including the location of the copy machines, the school calendar, their obligations for the year, lists of team members and important phone numbers. Sometimes the most basic things are not obvious to people who already call the school home, like where are all the bathrooms, and which are the most private? Your orientation is best spread out over a few days, and please always include food.

Start stopping by the new teachers' classrooms for quick visits early in the year. Afterwards, speak to them or email them a few positives you observed. If there are any red flags, for example, the behavior of the students is too casual and too chatty (a rookie mistake), you can nip it in the bud and give them the support they need. As anyone who has ever been a teacher knows, you can't put the discipline toothpaste back in the tube once it's out, but if you catch it early, you can jam it back in there.

Also remember that every event, whether it be parent teacher conferences or doing report cards, is new to them, even if they have taught elsewhere, so remind their mentor to go over these things with them and possibly review with them yourself. Every building and district has its own lingo, so don't assume they are familiar with it. They will need to hear things more than once. If you hired a few teachers at one time, it's helpful to create an email group that you can use to send them information and encouragement.

MBWA: MANAGEMENT BY WALKING AROUND

This is a crucial element of leadership that everyone seems to know about, but not always make time for. Everyone can be guilty of this, and sometimes an entire day will go by where you're stuck in your office, because as soon as you stand up to walk out, another person is standing there, or another phone call or email needs attention. If you do end up not walking around one day, you should try to make up for it the next day by visiting more classrooms and talking to more students than you normally would.

You may not have realized that MBWA was a coined phrase unless you've read *Gardening in the Minefield* by Laurel Schmidt,[1] probably one of the best school leadership books ever written, along with *The Challenge to Care in Schools*[2] by Nel Noddings. When you walk around, be interested and polite and don't interrupt classes or ask them to stop what they're doing. It seems to be easier to just "pop in" in a high school setting—in elementary school, they still want to chant in a singsong voice, "Good mor-ning!"

At the beginning of the year, you can tell teachers that you will be stopping by often, not to check on them, but to help inform your work, and because you care about what is going on in the classrooms. It's the most important thing. You can also assure them that if they happen to be checking their email or correcting papers once in a while, you understand.

Hopefully all school leaders were teachers first, too, and you are also human, but if you walk into their classroom five times in a row and they are checking email and sitting at their desk, maybe consider that something might be off. Even the most cynical teachers will want you to witness something wonderful happening, so stop by often enough that they feel proud of whatever you witnessed. Even if you walk into an elementary school classroom during snack time, the teacher will come to you later and say, "Oh, I wish I had been doing something better when you came by!" So stop by again soon, but hey—snack time is a big deal . . . even for adults.

It is helpful to carry a little pad of paper around with you, and write down little notes about positive things you see, or even to take notes on your phone. Tell staff that these quick visits will only be positive, and then always email them later and write a sentence or two about something great that you saw; a little email goes a long way. You should also write emails to the teachers' aides, as they don't always get as much feedback as the teachers. Small things mean a lot.

TEACHER OBSERVATIONS

Observing your teachers in their classrooms is one of the most important responsibilities and frankly, honors of your position. You have the opportunity to affect their instruction, and in turn influence how students feel in their classroom, in the school, and in their lives. It is a privilege and should be seen as such, instead of a tedious chore that is taking up your time. Most people who have been teachers have most likely been observed by both types of principals, and you know how each feels. If you check your email or are not completely invested while observing a teacher, it's disrespectful.

That being said, it takes time and focus, when your mind is racing with all the other things you could be doing, but if you relax into it, it will be the best part of your day. First of all, you will need to be familiar with the observation and evaluation procedures of your district and school, unless you are working in a small private school. In that case, you can come up with your own procedures. Many of them may be borrowed from public districts, but you can also make them your own. Here are the basic components.

First you will want to meet with your teacher for a "pre-observation." This will be a short meeting, approximately 15 minutes or less, when they let you know what the lesson will be. You should provide the teachers with lesson plan templates, instruction areas (some examples to be detailed in the next section), and basic expectations and guidelines. At this meeting, it is helpful if they have already written up their formal lesson plan, but this is not necessary if they are still working on it.

You'll find that some teachers will complete a detailed 3–5-page lesson plan, while others may do the bare minimum. For a formal observation, it's important to know they are capable of completing a comprehensive plan, so make that your expectation. If they start to skimp on the one or two days they are being formally observed, then components of a good lesson may also devolve over time.

Next, you should share with them what will happen when you come into their classroom and afterwards. Please, please do not be late. You will be wanting to see how the teacher greets the students, sets up the lesson, and so forth, and if you are even a few minutes late, you will miss this, and they will feel shortchanged.

You may also want to ask them if there is anything specific you want them to observe or look for. This is something that is effective with veteran teachers who are working to improve in a specific area. It's also helpful to share with new teachers that having someone in the room often affects things like "wait time" (how long to wait for students to respond), so remind them to slow down and breathe.

During the observation, take notes on all areas of assessment. If it's easier to bring your laptop or iPad, that's fine, unless it will distract you. The students will also be pleased that you are visiting, and will want to do their best. The teacher will most likely be nervous, so do everything you can to make them feel comfortable. You want them to do their best while you are in the room. If something goes wrong, just laugh with them. Share with them that this one class is only an example of one day, and no matter how good or bad it is, the reality of their day-to-day instruction usually falls somewhere in between.

One very important thing to do when you leave the classroom is to say something positive to the teacher. We have all been there! If the principal leaves your classroom without saying a word, and you don't meet with them for a few days or even longer, it can be torturous, and no one needs that. Say something like this: "Great job today! I really liked how you engaged with your students," or fill in the blank with all positives and just a few ideas. "Let's meet in the next few days to go over it. I will email you some times that could work for both of us. Thank you!"

Saying something like this will lower their anxiety and make them feel good, and they will tell their colleagues that your visit went well, and being observed isn't that bad. Even the most veteran teachers will be apprehensive about a formal observation, especially if you are new to the school.

Leave the classroom, go back to your office, and look at the teacher's schedule, then email them offering a few time slots for the post-observation. In the email you can also repeat something positive and simple, such as "Good job today!" Every once in a while, things go horribly wrong, and that needs to be addressed, too, but for the most part, you are just providing ideas, minor adjustments, and most importantly, a chance to mirror what they are doing every single day. Teaching is not an easy job, and having someone reflect back all the good they do for students helps!

Set aside a full period for your post-observation meeting. This may be the one time a year that your teacher has uninterrupted time with you, so hold all calls and close your laptop. Usually your school will have a standard form that needs to be completed; some schools follow a "narrative style" where you will write down everything the teacher does, step by step. Sometimes a combination of the two is best, but you will find your own way, even if you are required to follow a specific form.

It's productive to begin by asking the teacher how they thought the lesson went. They are sometimes their own worst critics, and it seems to be helpful for them to share their impressions. It's also a good sign something did go poorly, but they are aware of it. After that, tell them all the positives you observed, and don't leave anything out.

These should also be included in your written report, and reading them aloud is powerful. Usually you will have one or two suggestions, and if they are substantial, it is helpful to offer specific professional development, or maybe help from a veteran teacher. It can also be very beneficial to ask teachers to visit one or two other teachers each year, not to offer criticism, but just to get a feel for other styles of teaching. At the end of the post-observation, both parties sign the report, and walk away—hopefully feeling good!

INSTRUCTION

There are many instructional models, checklists, and philosophies, and you will hone your own or those required of your district or school as you gain experience, and combine different aspects you view as important. Your experience and opinion matter, but so does that of the academic and instructional team at your school.

This checklist is something that you can all work on together, and once it's compiled, it should be shared with everyone, because what you all view as "good instruction" should not be a secret to anyone. It can also be constantly evolving, so it needs to be revisited by you and your team at least once a year. Here is a basic, non-exhaustive list:

Teacher Observation Checks

- Connection to previous lesson
- Explanation of how the class period will be organized
- Anticipatory set: making objectives clear; don't teach without an end goal
- Lesson structure: in a 40-minute class, it should be "chunked" into at least three different sections, possibly including lecture, group work, multimedia, pair work, and practice. Students remember 5 percent of what the teacher says, but 90 percent if they're directly involved
- Checking for understanding throughout the lesson—individually and as a whole class
- Does the teacher have specific knowledge of students, including any special needs (IEP or 504 accommodations)? If so, do they implement them discreetly? Are barriers removed and adaptations provided for *all* students?
- Use of technology and instructional resources
- Clarity of oral and written communication
- Classroom environment: do they feel comfortable and safe?
- Are classroom procedures and rules clear and consistent?
- Practice of new material/scaffolding of content
- Wrap-up of lesson
- Classroom management
- Relationship with students/mutual respect
- Inclusivity of all students as individuals, taking into account their backgrounds
- Tone and style of teaching
- Content knowledge and passion
- Differentiation of material

- Student engagement
- Questioning techniques (not only calling on students with their hands raised)
- Sufficient wait time (this can be challenging when being observed)
- Fostering higher-level thinking and problem solving
- Sincere positive and constructive feedback—individually and as a whole class
- Organization of physical space
- Assessment of student learning
- Flexibility
- Conclusion: explanation of homework and what will come next, both next class and in the big picture. How does this isolated lesson fit into the whole?

Another part of your observation form should include things that cover whether the teacher is a good employee and team member, and participates in student life outside the classroom.[3]

Pedagogy
- The instructor has demonstrated appropriate and effective instructional and presentation strategies of the courses he/she teaches.
- The instructor provides appropriate and timely assessments and evaluations of student performance.
- Students in the instructor's courses have demonstrated appropriate academic achievement as measured by testing results and quarterly grades.

Professional Responsibilities
- The instructor completes and submits lesson plans or other required planning materials in a timely fashion.
- The instructor maintains and updates his/her teacher web page [such as Google Classroom] as required.
- The instructor's attendance and punctuality is acceptable.
- The instructor satisfactorily completes his/her proctoring responsibilities, such as maintaining a presence in the hallway between classes, homeroom duties, or other assigned proctoring responsibilities.
- The instructor regularly attends faculty and committee meetings.

Extracurricular Involvement
- The instructor is appropriately involved in extracurricular activities as required by the school contract.

ADMINISTRATIVE TEAM

The makeup of your administrative team can either make every day great, or every day drudgery; if you have any choice in the matter at any time in your career, choose wisely. All school leaders, at whatever level, come to the team with either no experience, differing experiences from different schools, or a lot of veteran-level experience.

If you have a team member, whether it's a principal, assistant principal, dean of students or discipline, any director, a vice president, or whatever the title, that has an ego and needs credit for everything, you are doomed.

The success of the team should be your number one objective, because that in turn affects the teachers, the students, and the school itself, so that is an important criterion to pay attention to when choosing members. Also, days get crazy and you need calm members and good communicators, and team members who don't feel slighted if you forget to share every detail about every single thing every second. Eventually all information gets shared.

It's good to have fun people, too, who can lighten things up and laugh at the crazy stuff. Choose people you would walk through fire with, and who would do the same for you. Easy, right? Then set up a daily or regular "touch base" meeting and take it from there. It's important to truly value and rely on assistants, because sometimes that job is more challenging than being the leader—the work is often tedious and in the weeds, with none of the glory.

NOTES

1. Schmidt, *Gardening in the Minefield.*
2. Nel Noddings, *The Challenge to Care in Schools: An Alternative Approach to Education* (New York: Teachers College Press, 2005).
3. St. Francis High School, "Non-Tenured Faculty Observation/Evaluation Form" (Hamburg: Administration, 2011).

Chapter 7

Students

Most people enter the field of education because of the students, so all that you do should begin and end with them in mind. You are shaping lives and influencing their future as human beings. What could be more important? The specifics of that work take time, experience, and work from both your head and your heart.

SPECIAL EDUCATION

Your school and/or district will employ specialized directors, teachers, and staff to oversee and implement a special education program for your students. That being said, it is also necessary for you to know the regulations, timelines, laws, and practices, but more importantly, for you to understand that each child, regardless of their disability or physical, mental, or emotional challenges, has the opportunity to achieve their fullest potential, and have access to the same education and opportunities that every child does.

How do you become an expert in special education? Some people will already have a background or degree in this area, and some of you will not, so you need to begin by studying the laws and regulations in your state and region.

In 2004, the Individuals with Disabilities Education Act (IDEA) was revised (originally PL 94–142) because half of the children with disabilities in the United States were not receiving appropriate educational services. IDEA is the main federal funding statute governing children from birth to age 21, and guarantees a FAPE (Free Appropriate Public Education).

The specific sections you will need to understand include part 200 (Students with Disabilities), part 200.3, which outlines the committee on special education, and part 200.4, which outlines the procedures for referral, evaluation, IEP development, placement, and review. You should also familiarize yourself with the basic definitions of services in speech, psychology, OT, PT, counseling, social work, mobility, and so on.

The guidelines and timelines for students and families with special education are extremely specific, and you are bound by law to follow them. You can use all the heart and empathy you have to support them, but there are also strict standards that must be followed to ensure equity in every aspect of their education.

The research regarding early intervention will help you support parents who are beginning the evaluation process for their child. Also remember that it's never too late for a child to be evaluated, and to receive appropriate supports and/or medication. Sometimes it doesn't happen until high school or even college, and that's ok, too. Navigate this process with love and information, and rely on the experts in your school.

WORK WELL WITH PARENTS

Many school leaders are blessed to have children of their own, and while it is certainly not a prerequisite of the job, it certainly helps when navigating the world of working with parents. Having a child or children can make you a better teacher, as well as a better school leader. It can provide you with empathy and understanding you could only have read about in books, or seen in movies, which is something to be incredibly grateful for.

Of course, there are lots of great teachers and school leaders who don't have children, but if you do, it can allow you to draw on your own experience, and your own personal stories. Over the years, it has become clear that even the most experienced and confident parents are looking for advice and support in many areas. Sometimes teachers don't realize that the things that are second nature to them may be foreign to parents not working in education.

Whether you have children or not, in all things it helps to provide personal insight, but more importantly, and most importantly, it helps to rely on the research. You can always be reading current research and sharing it with parents. Over the last few years, a compilation of research that has helped parents greatly with high school students is a textbook called *Adolescence*, by Laurence Steinberg. You can share things like examples of good parenting styles[1] through newsletters and at large meetings, as well as in individual one-on-one meetings.

In a high school setting, one of the most important research-based ideas you can share is that the brain of an adolescent is telling them to push parents away. Their brains tell them it's time to become independent, but in reality, they need us more than ever. It's a tricky dance, and parents need to put emotions and hurt feelings aside so they can set expectations, to be consistent, but also firm and loving. Once the parents of a high school student realize that their child has a natural urge to push them away and grow in independence, it is somehow easier to handle the distance and slights from them.

This style of parenting and teaching is called "authoritative." It makes sense that being firm and loving also describes the best style of teaching. Specifically, and according to the research, this is characterized by being child-centered, democratic, and flexible; establishing firm behavioral guidelines; engaging adolescents in decision making; being warm, accepting, involved and trusting; and supporting assertiveness, responsiveness, self-regulation, and psychological autonomy.[2] Easier said than done, but you get the idea.

It's also useful to share with the parents of adolescents that, contrary to popular belief and Freud's view of detachment, the current research (including some that was actually completed by Freud's daughter), shows that most families actually get along during their adolescent years, with their relationships and bonds intact.[3]

Another philosophy that is helpful, especially when working with challenging parents, is one where "everybody wins." This doesn't mean that you have to "give in" or change your policies or expectations because a parent disagrees with you; usually they just want someone to listen to them.

You should never shy away from these meetings or phone calls, because eventually you will discover that what they want, and actually need, is someone to listen to them. Many times it's important that that someone is you. If there is a conflict in a conversation, a phrase that can be helpful is, "It sounds like we want the same thing," or, "It sounds like we're saying the same thing." This can be disarming and take down walls.

It's also incredibly important to support your teachers, even if you disagree with something that happened. In that situation, you can still be honest with the parents, and say something like, "He should not have said that, or done that, but I'll talk to him, find out what happened, and fix the situation." Usually the "truth" is somewhere in the middle, but being honest (without throwing anyone under the bus) is effective in these meetings. Veteran leaders know that every time an angry parent calls or shows up at their door, they have an opportunity to make things right, simply by listening and talking to them in person.

Not all meetings with parents are negative. In fact, most are very positive, and the more effort you put into building relationships with them, the fewer negative meetings you will have. There are a lot of ways to get to know them before problems arise. You can have monthly coffees where everyone is invited, or one grade level, or half of the alphabet at a time. You can meet them at social events, and also set up regular parent meetings for them as a group.

Try to offer opportunities at different times of the day, as well as online conferences. Of course, it's preferable if a parent makes an appointment to see you, and you don't want to necessarily set a trend, but don't shy away from the parent that just pops into the school, and asks if you have a moment. Spend about 10 minutes with them, and don't feel bad if you cut it short. If there is a bigger issue, set up an appointment at another time.

ADOLESCENCE

Adolescence begins at puberty and ends when an individual assumes adult roles in society, so it can be a very long period of time, much longer than it was 100 years ago. School leaders working with adolescents will need to have specialized knowledge and experience. As stated in the aforementioned book *Adolescence* by Lawrence Steinberg,[4] there is important research that every principal needs to understand.

Working with this age group, which can span anywhere from fifth grade through college, carries with it many generalizations and misconceptions, but if you arm yourself with current research, you will be well-equipped to help your students, their parents and families, and their teachers.

Steinberg divides the research into biological, cognitive, and social transitions, and also takes into account the settings of families, peer groups, schools, and work and leisure. As noted earlier, this time period is when students have a natural tendency to push adults away, when actually they need adults more than ever. There is also a common misconception that mood changes are mostly due to hormones in adolescents, but research shows they are actually based on activity changes throughout their day that they don't have any control over. Hormones of course play a part, but the stereotype that teenagers are ruled by their "raging hormones" is simply not true.

Research in these areas can now show brain activity that increases risk taking tendencies when teenagers are together, as well as shedding light on the emotional issues that young people need to navigate and deal with, with an ever increasing social media presence in their lives. Both teachers and parents will tend to guide children the way they were guided, which is generally a good thing, but giving them some research about this age group can really help them.

As mentioned earlier, Dr. Leonard Sax is also an expert on adolescents, in addition to his work on gender, and his resources can be helpful. Anyone that has ever taught middle school has probably already developed strategies that support and help their students become their best selves, all while dealing with peer pressure and identify issues, along with possible burgeoning mental health issues. Kids truly need us more than ever at this age, and you need to be loving, firm, consistent, and available for them.

DISCIPLINE

Every mistake a child makes is an opportunity for growth. If you think back to the research cited above regarding how long it takes their brains to fully develop, this may help you understand their decisions and actions. It doesn't mean their lack of brain formation is an excuse for mistakes, but it can be an explanation. Also, anyone familiar with the stages of moral development will understand the different rates children develop a moral compass, along with both internal and external loci of control.

How you approach discipline in your school can have a big effect on the tone, and on the positive identity of your students. You don't need to be "punitive" or "catch" students being bad. This is the philosophy of some educators and disciplinarians, referred to as "authoritarian" parenting or educating. It's a "my way or the highway" mentality, where no gray area ever exists, and there is no room for discussion or explanation.

Anyone who was parented or disciplined in this style will remember it, and probably already realize that, as the research shows, it is extremely ineffective. You can put that in the same category as corporal punishment. It doesn't work. It often just teaches children to avoid the person dishing out the punishment, and can actually increase their oppositional behavior.

You will hopefully have a staff member as part of your team that specifically handles discipline, or in many schools, this will fall to the assistant principal, or the principal. If you can hire someone to delegate it to, their philosophy is extremely important, and then you can work together. If it falls to you, gather all the information you can, then meet with involved students, and listen. Once you have listened to everyone, you can decide on a consequence that is appropriate, and inform parents and students.

Every decision should be individualized, but also made after checking what was done in the past and what is outlined in the student handbook. The handbook should have some built-in room for discretion in its wording, but it is also a legally binding document. Consistent expectations are what are needed most. If you handle situations fairly and with love and support, students will serve their consequence, hopefully learn from the incident, and not repeat that exact mistake again.

NOTES

1. Steinberg, *Adolescence,* 104.
2. M. Martin, S. Basco, and P. Davies, "Family Relationships," in *Encyclopedia of Adolescence*, eds. B. Brown and M. Prinstein (New York: Academic Press, 2011), vol. 2, pp. 84–94.
3. Steinberg, *Adolescence*.
4. Ibid.

Chapter 8

Everyone

As noted above, some areas of school leadership are best handled with your heart, and others with your head, while some require both. This last area of head and heart work combined includes those areas that ultimately affect everyone you serve, as well as the overarching scope of your work.

SELF-FULFILLING PROPHECY/EXPECTATIONS

The idea of a "self-fulfilling prophecy" is one that has been around for a long time, but based on the research, and our own experiences as teachers, students, and, well, humans, this cannot be stressed enough. Teacher expectations have a big influence on how students feel about themselves and their academic success.

This applies to teachers as well as students; the more you believe they are wonderful, and communicate this to them, the more they *will* be wonderful! Think back to a time when someone had high expectations of you, and remember how it made you feel, and in turn, how it made you behave and perform in school, and in your world. It only takes one adult to believe in each child, and you can be that person to many. What an incredible responsibility and opportunity!

SPEAK WELL

There will be many events where you are expected to say something, and this is one of the easiest ways you can reach people, make them feel welcome, and make a big impact in setting the tone for who you are and what your school stands for. This is probably easier said than done. Sometimes you will succeed a school leader that shied away from speaking, because they were either nervous, or not good at it, or couldn't be bothered.

If this is the case, change that precedent immediately. Take the plunge and tell your staff, or the coordinators at any and every event, that you would like to say a few words, with emphasis on "a few." This has nothing to do with ego, so don't be afraid it will look that way.

Speaking at events follows the rule of being prepared in all things. Even if you are not scheduled to speak, have something very brief prepared. Someone may ask if you have anything to add out of respect. If you let the honest emotion in a little, but not so much that you do the ugly cry, then people will relate to it. They are emotional about their children and want to know that you care, too. You can have a few bullet points on an index card, or committed to memory, or in the notes app on your phone. Read the room.

Over time, you will realize that parents, as well as your own teachers and staff, just want to hear a few honest and heartfelt remarks. They want you to tell them that they are beautiful and valued and won't all be good at everything. Even if what you say seems small, if it's delivered with honesty and emotion, it can mean the world. If moms, dads, guardians, and grandparents don't cry at graduation and important occasions, then you haven't done your job.

Speaking at a school is a huge honor, and there is so much emotion and pride packed into school that it is a privilege. These ideas for speeches will come to you when you least expect it—in the shower, while driving, perhaps while running—so always have something to write on and with, and then sleep on the ideas, and they will write themselves. It's helpful to bring along a note card with bullet points so you are prepared, but can also sound like you are talking off the cuff. Practice, practice, practice and soon you will be able to spontaneously speak at every occasion.

WRITE WELL

Along the same line as remarks or speeches, it is very important to take the time to put things in writing for your school community, whether it be a regular newsletter, a monthly update, a graduation goodbye, or an email about a school event. It is an honor to write anything on a monthly basis that tries to tap into what parents might be feeling and thinking. Again, being a parent yourself can be invaluable here. They just want the truth and to know they are not alone. Take the politics out of your newsletters . . . leave that to someone else.

BE EQUITABLE

Before the next section on DEI and belonging, it is important to talk about equity within your school community, and before a discussion about matters of diversity, equity, inclusion, and belonging as they pertain to students, it is important to address basic equity and fairness in working with your teachers and staff. All of us have had the experience of having a boss who treats people differently, favoring some over others, and leaving you confused as to how to get the things you need, and how to please the boss. This isn't good, and it's the sign of a bad leader.

It's inevitable that you will have favorite people as a school leader. After all, human beings are going to be attracted to others who shine brighter (personal taste), and share similar sensibilities and lifestyles. All that being true, your teachers should never *feel* that you favor someone over them, or that you have a personal relationship with someone that could imply they may get more—more time, more attention, more resources, and so on.

Leaders need to work very hard at this, and be aware of their behavior and comments at all times. This is why not giving out special favors, financial opportunities, and pay increases is so important. Remain consistent in all things, and your true "favorites" or "friends" will understand and respect you for it. Find a way to make every person feel like they are your favorite.

DIVERSITY, EQUITY, BELONGING, AND INCLUSION

Some may call these "buzzwords," but hopefully most will know that focusing on diversity, equity, inclusion, and belonging in schools is long, long overdue. If you haven't participated in a book study, attended professional development on the topic, been to a seminar, listened to a guest speaker, or read another book (or two), then you need to start.

Everyone needs to continue working to give all students equitable opportunities, resources, and treatment, and to give teachers the tools, training, and support to improve in this area. A particularly low-hanging fruit is to address every racially charged comment in the classroom immediately. Teachers also need to examine their comments and behavior with colleagues, and keep each other honest. Continue working toward classroom environments where all students are valued and respected, and where the curriculum reflects their world. Time is up.

POST-COVID

Psychologist Dr. Pam Cantor was asked to conduct research after 9/11 on children who had experienced trauma. She was again asked to conduct research after the first year of the COVID-19 pandemic, for the same reasons. New school leaders who began their position in 2022, and were never involved in education, have been heard asking why everyone is still so stressed. School leaders need to understand that teachers and students are still stressed because COVID has not yet ended.

While no one can argue that everyone gained invaluable skills during these last two years, education will never be the same. This is a good thing in some respects, but school leaders need to be tuned in to what it means to be a teacher (and a student) during these times. Nothing will ever be the same. Cantor's research demonstrated that cortisol is secreted in times of stress, and the biggest remedy for that stress, and really the only thing that decreases it, is oxytocin; and the biggest transmitter of oxytocin is the human relationship. It is physiologically proven, and nothing else works. How fortunate everyone is to have something so powerful and free at our disposal.

Conclusion

So, in conclusion, if you are not already a kind, honest, and hardworking person who is educated, experienced, and knowledgeable and who genuinely cares about the people you are working with, then you had better learn to fake it, or get into a different field of work!

Appendix
Red Journal Entries and Musings

You have truly been such an inspiration and a gift to us and to me personally. Your energy, strength, professionalism and spirit can never be replaced—it was truly an honor to work for and with you each and every day.

MOST POPULAR

Even though everyone wants to be loved, it has never been my objective to be loved at work, or to be popular, because everyone knows that as a boss or a parent, that leads nowhere. I have always wanted to inspire employees to be their best selves, so they can do their best work, and in this case, influence students. I really believe that many of these leadership ideas can be applied to other administrative roles.

As an aside, I was voted most popular in high school, but I think it was for reasons that were not based on textbook "popularity." I think it was the basis for my leadership style today, and if I could sum up my style in a few words, they would probably include "respect" and "kindness." I try to treat people with respect and kindness because that is how I would like to be treated . . . the golden rule.

Based on everything my parents and family taught me, along with a few good teachers and bosses, and also some really bad ones (you need to have those bad ones to help you along the way, and I have had some doozies), I have realized that treating others with respect and kindness goes a very long way, possibly further than almost anything else.

> *I do know that my life is better with you in it. This is a better place for having you in it. You brought the best out in us and me personally. I never worked so hard and had such a good time doing it. Thanks for your gentle prodding, family-style leadership and for being you!*

LEAVING THE NEW YORK STATE RETIREMENT SYSTEM

I think that my "dissection" of and reflection on my leadership style began in a negative way. After eight years of teaching eighth grade English (AIS) in the same public middle school, I took a career risk and accepted a job as the principal of my high school alma mater. I can't really say that I chose to leave teaching, but rather that leadership chose me. I was told I was crazy to leave the New York State retirement system, and I guess that in some ways, I was, but apparently, that loss hasn't meant much to me because I seem to keep doing it.

I seem to keep taking risks and acting like I am a 25-year-old beginning my career over and over again. I keep forgetting that I am 50, and even when my urologist said last year, "Wow . . . that's pretty great, Lou . . . getting a public school principal position at your age," I know he meant it as a compliment, but I left my appointment thinking, "Who is he talking about? What age? How the hell old am I?" I guess it has never really caught up with me that the way I feel may not be the way I look, and is certainly not the age I actually am. . . . but maybe that's why I continue to be successful. Well, successful in my own way.

> *You have the enviable ability to put your colleagues at ease immediately and naturally. You created an atmosphere for working here at once professional and relaxed. The environment of the building was enhanced by your unassuming, sincere and most competent leadership. With gratitude and sincerity.*

ALMA MATER

Ok—so I get to my alma mater (where my four sisters and I attended high school) and there are so many wonderful things in place . . . for the most part. There are wonderful students, families, teachers, religious leaders, and staff. There is a wonderful, supportive community. That being said, there are so many things wrong at this school that my first year of planning to observe, absorb, and learn about the place is challenging.

It's a mess of the biggest proportions, and I know what a mess looks like, and what it does not, so I dive in and begin to fix it. I hire some really great people, rely on the great ones already there, and unfortunately, get rid of some "dead weight," which I believe is not a technical term, but anyway . . . I begin to change the tone of the school with some simple things. The whole place begins to respond. The reputation of the academy grows, as does enrollment, and with the current financial situation not really affecting us, people give more, do more, and it's all good . . . but then, suddenly, it's not again.

> *More important than any boss, you are a true friend. You are genuine, compassionate and truly care about the students and the staff. Test scores were secondary, but the true child was what mattered to you, along with the true people, not just the staff/teacher roles. Thank you so much for a wonderful year, for genuinely caring for both me and my family. Plus, you have awesome taste in music! Love,*

HAPPY BOAT

One thing you need to realize is that when you come into a place and change things, there are people who don't want to change. When you get more and more people on your happy boat, there will always be one or two people who get madder and madder, and some of these people are very good at poking holes in the boat. All their energy is spent trying to make it sink, and if you are naïve and trusting like I was, you don't even see it coming. You think the best of people, and once in a while, that can really bite you in the ass, and being bit in the ass can hurt.

> *Working with you and for you has been a true pleasure. Your genuine concern for each of us has made a difference. I am sure you will continue to make a difference in people's lives. The difference you make is positive and powerful. You are a special person, and truly unique. You are lucky to be you—so true to yourself. Peace.*

NEW BOSS

So I'm building this positive, successful culture, and they're running this underground game of their own. They have the ear of the religious community, the "owners" of the school, mostly because I don't realize part of my job should be defending myself—I didn't realize I was under attack. At the beginning of my third year, at the height of all things good, they bring over a new head sister as my boss. She's nice, she's fine, but I'm not sure why she's there, and I miss the last head sister, whom I respected and really liked. I soon find out her objective.

After two months, she says she is confused by my leadership style and asks if I could describe it to her. At this point, I have never been asked this question, and I'm not really sure how to answer. This begins the pivotal moment in my own journey of wondering what I am doing, and why it's making her so mad, since most everyone else loves my "style."

I tell her I can describe some of my practices, and I review one of my favorite leadership books, and I type up a list of things I strongly believe in and practice as a leader. She tells me that is not what she wants and she gives me a list of choices—old school styles. I am trying to please her, really, and choose one of these, but given the four categories, I can't really pick just one that defines who I am as a leader, so I take pieces from each and type up another response to discuss with her. She then takes a line from my precious "gardening" leadership book and sends it out to my staff, and asks them to describe my style in confidential responses to her.

> *This has been such a great year. You are so compassionate to the staff here! You understand that we work hard and that we do it for the kids! Also, you know we have lives outside of school and you understood when we had to leave to tend to our families. Most of all–you are who you are, what we see is what we truly get. You are one of a kind! Thanks for being so honest and kind to me this year. From one IA [my high school alma mater] girl to another, God bless you and your new journey! Much love,*

Well, now my happy staff at my alma mater is not so happy and feels I am being overly scrutinized, and just when the school is on a major upward swing, they question why this is happening. The teachers all fill out the form, except for the two or three undermining the happy boat (there will always be these people, no matter what and no matter where, and no matter who you are).

The teachers privately give me copies of what they wrote, including things like "brought our school to life, innovative, vivacious, extremely professional, consistently positive spirit and practice, intellectual and educational strengths, dedicated, caring, current, deeply devoted, honorable, sensitive, supportive, organized, equitable, efficient," and so on. So they are happy, and they are working harder than ever.

Now this is where things gets a little fuzzy. She meets with me and tells me that some of the staff are able to "somehow" work with this crazy style of mine, but the majority can't because it is not aligned with the mission of the school, and so their leadership group is going to have to decide what to do with me.

> *The most important thing about Lou is her loving heart. She is the world's best mom to Sam and inspires Tom to write romantic songs. She remembers everything about you and cares about your family. Lou wears her heart on her sleeve for the world to see. . . . but that's not what makes her real. She's laughter and light, kindness and care. But the most important thing about Lou. . . . is that she embraced us all! We'll miss you!*

(I can barely even stand re-reading these notes to type them here. I don't feel worthy, and to be honest, I feel sad. I am still mourning leaving these people and this experience. I still struggle with "God's plan for me." I accept it, but I don't always like it.)

GRATITUDE

Well, a lie is a lie, and the day a religious person lies to you is the day to run as fast as you can in the opposite direction. I do have to thank this particular person, because in very small and possibly large ways, she has pointed me in the right direction several times in my life. When I attended this school as a student, she was actually a guidance counselor. I met with her one time and one time only, and in that minute-long meeting about my future career options, she told me I could be a teacher, a nurse, or a mom.

I remember thinking, "Really? These are my choices? That's it?" Not that any of those choices are insignificant, but the scope of what she offered to me as a woman seemed to be. The positive side is that her limiting choices propelled me to keep striving to be the best I could be. Those words stayed with me.

She also told my youngest sister that she couldn't pursue a pharmacy degree, and she wouldn't allow her to take the necessary science courses, but my sister found a way to do it. She actually got my parents involved and fought to offer AP (Advanced Placement) courses, and they formed a committee and made it happen. I went back to my alma mater to change some of these things, but some things just can't be changed, and you have to learn to achieve in spite of it all . . . or because of it all.

If I had known what I was getting into, I wouldn't have taken the job. But if I hadn't taken the job, I wouldn't have received the gifts and experiences I have been blessed with, and for that, I am grateful, even to those who tried to hurt me. I have to let it go, move on, and pray for them. My alma mater actually closed several years after I left, so I guess their objective was accomplished. Sad, but true, and now there is not a Catholic, private, or all girls' school in our area without having to drive 45 minutes.

> *I wanted a perfect ending. Now I've learned, the hard way, that some poems don't rhyme, and some stories don't have a clear beginning, middle, and end. Life is about not knowing, having to change, taking the moment and making the best of it, without knowing what's going to happen next. . . . Gilda Radner.*

> *I have watched you this year share so much of yourself with all of us here. Your passion and kind heart have touched us all. You have a gift to connect with children and adults on such a genuine level. Your gracious, humble spirit allows you to accept people wherever they are. Your strong faith and grateful heart will make you a blessing to all those who know you. Thank you for all your support this year! Bye for now.*

MONTHLY MEETINGS

I won't go into specifics about the monthly meetings with this sister that led up to the final meeting, but let's just say that some of them were so demeaning and off-base that I would get into my little red VW bug, begin to drive home (a five-minute drive), and be crying so hard I would have to pull over on the side of the road. She would include the assistant principal in these meetings (someone I supervised), and berate me in front of her for hours. I once asked her how she could handle talking to someone like this, and not even being constructive. She said, "Oh this is nothing. I have done much worse."

The comments that stick out in my memory are when she asked me what "all the joy and energy" was about, as she didn't think it was appropriate in a Catholic all girls' school; when she said I wasn't "welcoming enough"; and when she said that no one in the school was happy since I came there. She said I was there in body but nothing else. I knew these words weren't true and were actually the exact opposite of the truth, but they hurt just the same. I knew she was wrong and misinformed, but it was her school, and I knew I would have to move on, even though the girls, their families, and the teachers wouldn't understand.

> *The highest form of wisdom is kindness- the Talmud. Thank you for your kindness. You bring humor, joy and wisdom to everything you do. You make each person feel special and appreciated. There is a balance between family and career. You have the intuition to realize this is important in everyone's lives. In one year, you have left an imprint on our hearts. Your strong faith and caring nature will be greatly missed. Fondly,*

RESIGNATION

A few days later, I was in the hall speaking to a student at her locker and I cut my conversation short, remembering that she had told me to stop counseling students and talking to them when they were disciplined, and just to give them the consequence and move on. I changed who I was at that moment, and I didn't like who I could become, just to please her. I knew that what I was doing was important, and I had to move forward and continue my work. It broke my heart that I couldn't do it in the high school that my four sisters and I had attended, but I knew God had a plan for me to move on, and I was right. As per my contract, I had to give 90 days' notice.

It is still heartbreaking to remember that day because she made me get up in front of the entire student body and tell them I was leaving, which was followed by months of them asking me to lie to the school community, the school board, and others. I was professional and never spoke my truth, but maybe I should have. Maybe that's why I am telling it here. I realize that my story is small compared to the unjust experiences of so many people in the workplace, but it's my little story to share.

I worked until the end of my contract, which was June 30, and on June 28, I was finally offered a new position. It was only a substitute position, but one I needed and loved. It confirmed that I was onto something . . . something very big about being a leader.

> *You know you are going to be missed dearly by all of us. Your joy, your laughter, and your genuine kindness will always remain in our hearts here.*

WILCO

One morning I woke up in North Adams, Massachusetts, on a very rainy, foggy morning in the Berkshire Mountains. I am here with my husband Tom and our son Sam, and we are going to spend three days at a music festival, hosted and headlined by one of our favorite bands, Wilco. I am looking out the window of this old, red-sided motel at the beautiful mountains, and I say to my family, "This is the first time in four years that I have had a moment to think.... and to breathe.... and I am really wondering about my leadership style and what all the fuss is about."

What I am wondering is, what am I doing that is making people so happy to come to work? What am I doing that is increasing involvement, productivity, and job commitment and satisfaction? Is it conscious or unconscious? Can it be dissected, explained, taught, written about, and described?

> *I've learned that people will forget what you said, people will forget what you did, but people will NEVER forget how you made them feel ... Maya Angelou. Please know I will NEVER forget. All the best as you begin a new journey.*

CLASS PRESIDENT

In 2006 I earned a second master's degree in Educational Leadership, and while I came across certain little practices I would adapt and make my own, most aspects of my leadership "style" were things I developed when I was the senior class president. I remember the time before I ran for president that year, and since I had been an officer each of my three years thus far, I didn't want to run. I wanted to give someone else the office.

My classmates were trying to persuade me to run, and I remember having a conversation with my parents and saying I didn't want to "hog" the office. They asked if I could do a good job, and I said, "Probably." They said that if I could be a good leader to my classmates then it was my *responsibility* to run, and so I did. I think that was the first time I realized that if you have certain strengths, you need to use them. That's what God put us here for; at least that's what I believe, and hopefully it will be something that feeds you, too.

I have repeated this concept to countless students when talking about leadership. Leadership comes in different forms. Sometimes it's quiet and sometimes it's more overt, but students can usually name who their class leaders are, and they can also identify whether they are hiding their own talents and letting others take all the risks.

I know that even in my most exhausted moments of being a school leader–because doing the job well can be completely exhausting–I love being in a position to be welcoming and able to influence how people feel being part of a school community; being able to set the tone. I feel honored to represent a community, and to influence how its members feel about it. As I learned at my alma mater, it's great to be the boss and be able to lead, but it only works if you have a team that believes in the same message and has the same philosophy.

> *It has been AMAZING working with you! From the very first letter you sent us back in August, I could tell you were someone special. Little did I realize how special! Your genuineness, compassion, sentimentality, and sense of humor will be missed by everyone! Wishing you every happiness!*

MIDDLE MANAGEMENT

After being a principal for four years, I was now an assistant, which brought new challenges and lessons. I've learned over the last eight years that when you are not the principal, you can affect the tone of the school in many important ways, and you can fill in gaps and offer support, but it's definitely different. I have realized that the part I miss about being the principal is that by virtue of your office alone, the tone you set carries more weight.

If you show up to a basketball game as the principal, it "weighs" more than if you show up as the assistant principal. It's difficult to explain, and I struggled with this new role for a while. For a few years, it sometimes made me feel like I wanted to pursue a new principal position, and maybe I should have, but I never did because I felt loyal to this new community. As a result, I learned new lessons. I learned how to be part of a support team, and I learned how to work with different styles of leadership. My principal and boss was younger than me, and was beginning his twenty-seventh year at the school. We were very different in our leadership styles, but intersected when it came to doing what is best for students—the most important thing.

So we're in the Berkshire Mountains, and it rains all weekend, like a glorious muddy Woodstock, and I grab the printouts from our ticket registrations and start to write. We stop at a drugstore, and I buy a pen and paper and continue to write. After a weekend at the Wilco festival, a week in Cape Cod, and then two days in Manhattan (we like to mash up the yin and the yang all in one trip), I came home and typed all this up. After a lifetime of leadership roles and honing my "style" and practice, I realized that I might actually have something to say.

You have been such a blessing for me and this building. Your kind, caring, and sincere ways have been contagious, and you have made a positive impact on all of us. I am going to miss terribly your spirit, quick wit, thoughtful approach to problems, sense of calm in moments of crisis, unrelenting support, and extraordinary ability to make people feel loved and cared about. St. Francis is so lucky to have you! You are one of those people who you cross paths with once in a lifetime, but your influence on me will be a lasting one. Love,

SCARED

The reason I am scared to take over this position for a year is that the woman taking the leave of absence is perfect, and I'm not, so I'm wondering what I'm going to do to measure up. She is young (more than ten years younger than me), she is beautiful (and blond), she runs marathons (I have since run three half marathons, so maybe that equals a whole), she was the principal there for seven years, and she has already completed her doctorate!

She doesn't have children, so I rationalize that taking some time to raise my son, proudest accomplishment, is why I am so far behind in other areas. She is the ultimate professional, a stylish dresser, and someone I admire greatly, and I am realizing I am never, ever going to measure up.

I stop in the school a week before I begin, have a pleasant and very positive experience visiting with the two office secretaries, and promptly go out into the parking lot and hit someone's car. In my defense, I am in my husband's large jeep, and I am nervous and excited and don't have the best spatial perception, and I hit it so hard that their car alarm starts going off. I am mortified! Now somehow, by the grace of God, there was no damage, but at this point, I haven't even started the position, and I have to go back into the school only to find out that it's the car of my new administrative assistant!

Dear Lou—it sounds so common, and yet, it describes you perfectly. You have become so dear to my heart–and to all of those who have spent this year with you. You have a wonderful gift, Lou. Your gift is that you care so much for your family (Tom and Sam are so blessed to have you), your friends (and you make everyone your friend!), and each person who crosses your path. You believed in me, you cared about me, and you inspired me to give all of myself, and to do all that I could do for those around me. You are such a blessing–one I will always remember fondly. I pray that our paths will cross again someday soon. May God continue to use you and to bless you until then . . . Love,

MORTIFIED

So that begins my time at Eggert Road Elementary School. I don't actually officially begin the position until the following week, so there is still more damage to be done. Two days later, on Friday, one of the administrators from the district calls and leaves a message on my cell phone, asking me to join the entire administrative team at a three-day out-of-town conference in a week. I am nervous and can't imagine staying with (mostly) strangers for the weekend when already I barely think I will be able to handle this job, so I call him back and leave a message politely declining.

This becomes the second mortifying experience at a job I have not even begun. The same day I leave home to have lunch with friends, and go outside to get in my husband's jeep. There is no gas . . . it's below empty, and I am already late. I let out a few swear words, and then go back into the house to get the keys to my car.

I get into my car and there are two flat tires . . . you can't make this stuff up. I swear some more—never said I was a saint—and then my husband and son come out to help me pump up the tires . . . I am swearing, then yelling how much I love them . . . a million crazy emotions in two minutes. . . . I get in the car and begin singing (loudly) to a favorite song.

> *Our community has been blessed by your kind heart and pure generosity of spirit. You are not a person that can be replaced, but the goodness you have left behind will always be remembered. Many thanks for all of your kindness to me. There are so many treasures just waiting to be opened. Your message to me about listening to God was just what I needed. I do believe that God will put me exactly where I need to be, and he has clearly held you in the palm of his hands through your journey.*

On my way to lunch, I glance at my phone to make sure my friends haven't texted and I see I have "butt dialed" the previous call I made, and it's still recording . . . you guessed it . . . four minutes of my swearing/loving/singing. . . . all being recorded on the administrator's phone. I don't even know how to explain this to my family. I call them crying . . . I call my mom, too, and I decide I need to just resign before I begin. I am never going to measure up. I am never going to be able to work in a public school as a principal. My mom and husband and son all echo similar messages to me:

Just because you have (already) made a fool out of yourself and just because you are not perfect and you never will be, you are going to keep this job, because you need a job! The moral is that even though you make mistakes and your last boss didn't like you or even "get" you, you are going to be yourself, because that's all you have. And so I began. On the first official day of school, speaking to my 100 new staff members, I wasn't nervous at all.

I was excited, happy, and comfortable, and exactly where I was supposed to be, and in many ways, that's because the 100 people looking back at me at our opening meeting were very much like me. We were honest, we were hardworking, and we were real. This leadership book is a description of a year I just spent surrounded by love and support, and realizing that my style was just fine.

> *I will never forget this year with you. It has been very special to me and you are one of the reasons it was so special. When you came in September, I immediately felt comfortable and close to you. I noticed your intelligence, fairness, and professionalism right from the start. You are a true educator, administrator, and champion for children!*
>
> *You have been one of the best administrators I have had the privilege to work for. Your exceptional administrative skills are really not what this letter is about. This letter is about how you were one of the few things that happened to me this year that opened the door to real happiness.*
>
> *Wow, that sounds pretty big. Well, I guess it is. Your warmth, caring, and acceptance have truly made this one of my best teaching years in a long time. I remember being at Tom's concert in the library around Thanksgiving and feeling so connected. Lou, you are a connector. Your transparency, your realness, your caring and compassion connect people together. That is a true gift. You are a true gift.*

Epilogue

Voices from the Field

Several school leaders have contributed their ideas about leadership:

Thomas Braunscheidel, High School Principal
Cindy Krug, Director of Guidance
David Lilleck, Superintendent
Matthew McGarrity, retired Superintendent
Paul Pietrantone, Director of Special Programs
Sue Schaffstall, Vice President of Marketing and Communications
Joan Thomas, retired Superintendent
Jonathan Wolf, High School Principal

THOMAS BRAUNSCHEIDEL, HIGH SCHOOL PRINCIPAL

In my view, educational leadership at any level or position is about relationships and the understanding of the culture and mission of the institution. Education occurs between and among people who all have a unique set of strengths, weaknesses, and talents. Relationships, in whatever state they exist, affect teaching and learning.

The school leader needs to understand the relationship among the faculty, staff, and administration and how it came to be, for better or worse. These relationships define the school's culture. Additionally, school leaders need to understand the stated mission of the school, and how that mission is understood by the school stakeholders.

The culture of any school includes many facets, including, but not limited to, the relationship between administration and all stakeholders (faculty, staff, students, parents, and the community), as well as the relationship of these groups with each other. Those relationships, and the culture that they form, reveal the priorities of the school and the level of harmony or discord that may exist. This culture may be a result of challenges and successes in the life of a school over time. Those challenges and successes may include student achievement; respect and compensation afforded to faculty and staff; student deportment; and community relations, among others.

The relationships and culture reveal strengths and weaknesses in the institution. With a sound understanding of school culture, a school leader can identify the dynamics of power and influence and what obstacles to anticipate as he/she attempts to act as a catalyst for change and growth. With the knowledge and understanding of current culture, a leader may leverage natural allies and help repair and tend broken relationships. Without an understanding of the school's culture, a leader may unintentionally blunder into mine fields that subvert the progress of the institution.

One incontrovertible part of education is change, for better or worse. Change can be positive and necessary, but is frequently uncomfortable. Amidst all the change, a school needs a consistent guiding focus that serves as the cornerstone that all change is built upon and referred back to. This cornerstone is the school's mission. The mission needs to be clearly articulated and understood by the stakeholders. It will guide school leaders both when change is thrust upon them, and when leaders recognize that it's time to promote needed change.

The mission statement remains when all else changes. It's what leaders reference when they make decisions about what is right or wrong for the school. School leaders need to help other stakeholders understand the mission, and how to refocus those who would set their own agenda apart from the stated mission.

The average tenure for a school principal is from four to six years depending on what source you reference. The average faculty and staff member will likely outlast most principals. Schools with high levels of leadership turnover can breed skepticism about the commitment of school leaders. Principals change for a variety of reasons. It is important for a new principal to understand the culture of the school and build relationships in order to lead. A leader needs to focus on the cause greater than themselves—the mission. With a focus on relationships, culture, and mission, a leader stands the best chance to effect positive change.

CINDY KRUG, DIRECTOR OF GUIDANCE

Student situations get complicated and there are often layers to uncover before you get to a solution. Instead of looking at the big picture and working down to the student, the opposite is more helpful. It's best to start with a student-centered approach, and determine what is most important to this individual. What lessons need to be a part of the plan? Who are the professionals in our school community that need to be aware and brought in on this? And then, how does this connect with the larger picture?

Everything in school leadership begins with communication and then develops into relationships: not only interpersonal relationships, but also the relationship the administration has with families, faculty, and, of course, students. If families feel that they aren't getting information consistently, they don't know how to trust what is happening at school. When faculty trusts that they know what is in the strategic plan of the school or district, they are better able to plan their curriculum and careers. Students need to know that they have people who truly care about them and are available to them, and this ultimately happens through the relationships they build.

It matters when administrators know how students and families feel about their experience. You see trends when you meet with multiple students who talk about the fact that they know their teachers care about them. They can identify multiple adults in the building that they would be comfortable going to when they need help.

This is accomplished through a culture of openness, caring, and concern, and it results in a unique school community. Leading from a place of open communication and modeling professionalism and competence gives students and families the security that they need to proceed through the demanding years of adolescence, knowing we are their safety net when they need it.

DAVID LILLECK, SUPERINTENDENT

Throughout all of my experiences, my leadership focus has been one based on service leadership, with a personal focus on faith-based leadership. My faith is central to my leadership. It is my guiding compass.

With this as the focal point of my leadership philosophy, I looked to harness and build relationships and trust in my people. Three words resonated as I worked to inspire, while at the same time calming the waters and reducing the noise that we are often faced with. These words are *grace, mercy, and perspective*.

If you strive to treat all people with grace, it allows you to lead without falling into power struggle traps. Leadership should never be about power. Life is challenging, and people make mistakes. Who am I to judge, lest I be in a similar situation in the future! Grace allows you to build trust. Mistakes will happen.

We are working with the most unpredictable asset available, but the most important and powerful—people! When a mistake or issue rises to the surface, you cannot shy away from the challenge, but rather you need to approach it through the lens of grace as you work to correct, support, and inspire positive outcomes. Without grace, trust cannot be fostered.

Mercy. Who has not made a mistake in their life? Mercy allows you to look at the world around you in a manner that shines a light on those who are in the darkness. It allows you to work to give voice to the voiceless. It allows you to establish an expectation of greatness, with an understanding that great things do not happen without trials and tribulations. As you look at your students and families, a sense of mercy allows the school community to look differently. Instead of obstacles and challenges, you see opportunities to assist others to grow and reach their true potential. It fosters empathy. It creates trust. It creates family.

Finally, by leading with a sense of grace and mercy, you will foster a clear perspective that is leading with the heart and with love. It allows you to see opportunities for you to be light and salt. You work to not become stressed when the things that are truly not important interrupt your day. Perspective allows you to be a thoughtful leader, not a leader who is running with their hair on fire.

As leaders, our job is to reduce anxiety, not to increase it. If you are overly stressed by a student situation, a parent situation, a mandate, or you simply allow the outside noise of the world to impact your response to your circumstances, you will pass that on to those you are leading. They will sense that, and trust will be impossible to fully harness. Anxiety and stress will grow.

Your perspective, when rooted in grace and mercy, will allow you to place the outside noise on its proper shelf and provide you with the daily strength and mental capacity needed to do the truly important work you must accomplish each and every day. And that work, rooted in grace and mercy, is centered on what is best for your students and their outcomes. That needs to be your perspective. Not the perspective of the outside voices, so often led by adults who are not coming from a place of grace and mercy.

This perspective has allowed me to keep coming back to a place of love for all. Each student. Each teacher. Each support staff member. Each family. Each community member. Even the most challenging members of your community; *especially* the most challenging members of your community! Grace and mercy allow you to have that perspective. It allows you to calm the waters and silence the noise as you work to inspire great things in your community.

MATTHEW MCGARRITY, RETIRED SUPERINTENDENT

I would say that the basis of my leadership philosophy would consist of strong relationships based on mutual trust. If these critical elements are in place, one can work through most, if not all, conflicts that may arise. In all positions, I have spent considerable time getting to know my board of education, staff, students, parents, and community members. I strongly believe that it is a leader's responsibility to help people love their job, no matter what that job is. Again, this comes from a place of genuine kindness and trust.

I also believe that when trust and relationships are in place, communication is clear and frequent, thus honoring peoples' time and professionalism. When staff work for a manager, they know what the manager needs. When staff work with a leader, the leader knows what the staff needs.

PAUL PIETRANTONE, DIRECTOR OF SPECIAL PROGRAMS

The foundation of my philosophy is always to make decisions based on the best interests of students. I found that there are occasions when people want you to make decisions because it makes things easier or the workload lighter. School leaders must stay steadfast in their approach and keep students at the center of their decision-making.

As a leader, there is a value in demonstrating vulnerability to the teachers in the school. It's ok for them to know that I don't always have all the answers, but I am willing to learn and collaborate. Some of the best professional development occurred when I sat next to teachers to understand what they were learning. This reinforced the concept that we were all learners, and that improvement is ongoing. Creating a collaborative, learning-focused culture is a significant part of the school principal's job. When the principal is a model of openness and honesty, teachers are more likely to have a collaborative relationship with one another.

The family-school connection is a relationship that the leader should thoughtfully foster and model for school faculty. As educators, we can't change what happens outside of school hours, but we can work hard to develop relationships with families so that communication becomes more accessible. Welcoming families into the school requires an intentional approach that considers parental perspectives on the school and lets them feel that they are valued partners.

A challenge for principals is the range of various perceptions about the role of the principal that people have. Some teachers and parents want and expect their principal to have an authoritarian style. *Can a principal be friendly and patient with students and still be a good principal?* I believe the answer is yes! Maybe their principal was stern when they were students, and that's what they knew.

Occasionally teachers want you to be tough on all behavioral issues, even when the student has unique challenges. It was not my nature or leadership style to throw the book at young students. Many students come to school with challenges that make school hard. I tend to give these students extra time and patience. Whenever I needed to make a phone call to a parent, I could sense the tension on the other end. I always attempted to make discussions about student discipline a learning experience for students, but nobody wanted a phone call from the principal.

SUE SCHAFFSTALL, VICE PRESIDENT OF MARKETING AND COMMUNICATIONS

I like to think of myself as a "lead by example" type of leader. I will never ask any member of my team to do something that I will not do myself. No matter the task, a good leader should be willing to pitch in when needed and roll up their sleeves.

In addition, I am not a "one size fits all" type of leader. Team members are individuals with distinct personalities and work styles. They do not all respond to the same management style, so getting to know team members is critical to learning what motivates them to do the best job possible for the organization. It is important to make sure that team members feel valued, and to give praise as well as constructive criticism when warranted.

JOAN THOMAS, RETIRED SUPERINTENDENT

When I was teaching college courses for teachers who wanted to become administrators, one of the early discussions each semester focused on the characteristics of a successful leader. We considered respect, trust, collegiality, relationship-building, knowledge, patience (the list goes on). However, in my opinion, the most important skill is the art of successful communication. Communication must be timely, earnest, and efficient. Effective communication also involves the ability to be an active listener. For you see, as I will show, communication may be more about listening than speaking. Often in my experience, listening may solve more problems than you could imagine.

Case in point: So you are sitting in your office. It is 4:00 p.m. at the end of a typically hectic, busy day. You are confronted with emails, texts, mail, and phone calls. Ugh! (One of my mentors told me never to leave any message unanswered.) So I begin with texts and emails, and read the mail trying to sort through and establish meaningful piles (and also to discard as much as possible) so that the next day I can begin again!

If I was lucky some of this correspondence could be handled throughout the day so as not to have too much later. However, your texting must never interfere with face-to-face conversations, meetings, or committee work. I think one of the rudest, most disrespectful activities is to be texting while in a meeting! Also, none of this should ever be done in lieu of being visible with teachers, kids, and parents throughout the day. Your office is for after-hours work, for the most part.

Anyway, after I finished with my social media "conversations," I would begin returning phone calls. I'm ready to listen and have a dialogue, but I hope to get an answering machine, at which point I respond, "This is Mrs. Thomas. I am returning your phone call. Please call back at your convenience or call my secretary tomorrow if you want to meet in person. Thank you, and have a good evening." Now I hope they don't call back, but the ball is back in the caller's court, and I've done my job by responding on the same day. (Document everything.)

Now let's consider what might happen if the caller answers the phone. I say, "Hi, this is Mrs. Thomas returning your call. How can I help you?" The caller then spends many minutes usually complaining about someone or something that has provoked him or her. At the conclusion, I say, "Ok, let me see if I understand the situation." I begin to reiterate their comments from my notes. This validates their concerns, shows that I was actively listening, and then I may say, "Is this correct?" and if it is, I say, "What do you want me to do?"

In 80 percent of the cases, the caller will simply say, "Nothing. I just wanted you to be aware." (Or something to that effect.) Then the conversation ends with a "thanks for your time, take care, and goodbye."

Happy ending all around. The important takeaway here is to call back immediately, listen without interruption, not become defensive, give value to their comments, and work together to find a solution. Communication like this works and your job becomes much less confrontational. Also, you feel you have accomplished a lot in the day, and you leave feeling fulfilled.

JONATHAN WOLF, HIGH SCHOOL PRINCIPAL

My leadership philosophy is centered on the importance of developing strong working relationships with all of the varied constituent groups that a school leader has the opportunity to interact with while performing their job duties. School leadership encompasses many different roles and responsibilities. Even the most experienced school leader cannot be completely prepared to respond to the many situations and challenges that arise on a daily basis on their own. Developing strong working relationships, and working cooperatively to arrive at the most appropriate and beneficial decisions is critical in effective school leadership.

Drawing heavily on my training as a school counselor, I have learned that strong communication skills are essential in developing any relationship. Working cooperatively with people requires one to actively listen, synthesize information, and ultimately express an understanding of what is being discussed. Relying on these skills has often helped me effectively navigate challenging situations.

In my experience, "just listening" has been extremely valuable in most situations. Whether it be in working with students, parents, or staff, simply listening to their concerns or position on a particular topic helps to take emotion out of the conversation. Once we have established an understanding of the true concern, we can begin working on solutions or a plan of action. When people feel like their input has been considered, even contrary decisions or plans can be more palatable.

Developing strong relationships also means that a school leader needs to be willing to consider opinions other than their own. Establishing a strong level of trust that each member of a group is invested in making the best decisions to achieve the collective goals is important. Leaders serve as the facilitators of these conversations and help guide the process, but must be willing to accept that their idea may not be the best. I frequently rely on my colleagues to help me process the ramifications of making a particular decision.

References

Carey, Benedict. 2015. *How We Learn: The Surprising Truth about When, Where, and Why It Happens.* New York: Random House.

Duckworth, Angela. 2016. *Grit: The Power of Passion and Perseverance.* New York: Scribner.

Dweck, Carol. 2006. *Mindset: The New Psychology of Success.* New York: Ballantine Books.

Frank, Thomas. 2019. "13 Essential, Science-Backed Study Tips." YouTube video. 12:33.

Frankel, David. 2006. *The Devil Wears Prada.* Fox 2000 Pictures.

Hsieh, Tony. 2013. *Delivering Happiness: A Path to Profits, Passion, and Purpose.* New York: Grand Central Publishing.

Jackson, Shirley. 1949. *The Lottery and Other Stories.* New York: Farrar, Straus, and Giroux.

Martin, M., S. Basco, and P. Davies. 2011. "Family Relationships," in *Encyclopedia of Adolescence*, eds. B. Brown and M. Prinstein. New York: Academic Press, Vol. 2, pp. 84–94.

Mischel, Walter. 2015. *The Marshmallow Test: Why Self-Control Is the Engine of Success.* New York: Little, Brown and Company.

Noddings, Nel. 2005. *The Challenge to Care: An Alternative Approach to Education.* New York: Teachers College Press.

Sax, Leonard. 2016. *Boys Adrift: The Five Factors Driving the Growing Epidemic of Unmotivated Boys and Underachieving Young Men.* New York: Basic Books.

Schmidt, Laurel. 2002. *Gardening in the Minefield: A Survival Guide for School Administrators.* Portsmouth: Heinemann.

St. Francis High School. 2011. "Non-Tenured Faculty Observation/Evaluation Form." Hamburg, New York: Administration.

Steinberg, Lawrence. 2023. *Adolescence:* 13th edition. New York: McGraw Hill.

Tovani, Chris. 2000. *I Read It but I Don't Get It: Comprehension Strategies for AdolescentReaders.* Portland: Stenhouse Publishers.

About the Author

Dr. Mary Louise Stahl has worked for over 30 years in education, as a teacher, principal, college professor, and writer. She spends her time hanging out with her husband Tom, their son Sam, and their Chihuahua Joe Fox, because they all "love New York in the fall"! This book is dedicated to her large extended family, and to all the school leaders who navigated COVID and still give their heart every day!

www.ingramcontent.com/pod-product-compliance
Lightning Source LLC
Chambersburg PA
CBHW032031230426
43671CB00005B/274